A Reason To Smile

A Reason To Smile

AFRICAN CARIBBEAN AFRICAN-AMERICAN

HISTORY
IN
POETRY

The Story of the Struggles, Sacrifices and Sufferings
of Africans
for Survival and Success in America.

LLOYD E. AFFLICK

authorHOUSE®

AuthorHouse™
1663 Liberty Drive
Bloomington, IN 47403
www.authorhouse.com
Phone: 1-800-839-8640

Published by AuthorHouse   11/26/2014

ISBN: 978-1-4772-6618-2 (sc)
ISBN: 978-1-4772-6617-5 (e)

Library of Congress Control Number: 2012916370

Contents

We Are One!!

Dedication

Dear Reader

Someone once said—
"You can't know where you are going
Unless you know from whence you came."
This is true—whether you are simple,
Or someone of great fame.

This work is dedicated to my wife and daughters two,
It is dedicated also, to you and your children too.
Poetry makes History a lot more fun;
There is something here, for everyone.

There are many students who don't understand,
How we came to inherit this beautiful land.
The stories here will simply explain
The inner workings of the colonial game.

Children of Africa, it's especially for you;
Here you will find much that is interesting and new.
Of Europe's contribution a lot is said,
But there is much about Africa, that you never have read.

Read this book with an open mind,
Much you might learn about mankind.
I am not an Oxford Don or a Harvard Fellow,
 Just think of me as your **Story Teller.**

Lloyd E. Afflick

Introduction to
The American Story

Day after day we are fascinated by the things we see,
The answers to our questions are embedded in History.
Sometimes our answers seem untrue,
Simply because of the facts we do not know.
Like Science, History deals with cause and effect,
But the conclusions we draw are sometimes incorrect.

The parts of the puzzle are sometimes to be found,
Between the pages, or buried six feet under the ground.
The more you read, the more you will see,
How our modern conditions came to be.
Here again, the American story is re-told,
Much you will discover as the story unfolds.

If all the parts we were able to find,
Then we could write the true story of mankind.
Man's desire to know his past,
Causes a search for truth, which forever will last.
History gives a pleasure of a special kind,
Which even the simplest reader will certainly find.

This work deals with the last 500 years,
Here you will share people's hopes and also their fears.
We begin at a time when life was 'slow'
About the world, very little did people know.
People did not move from place to place,
There was a separation of the human race.

Then change came at a rapid rate,
It was hard to keep track of historical dates.
Change came at that very hour
When people realized, that within, there was potential power.
No more were they by custom and tradition controlled,
The wonders of nature began to unfold.

It is most amazing when one stops to survey,
How in such a short time the world became this way.
From a time when sailors were guided by stars,

To a time when we are planning to visit Mars.
From a time when there was not even a printing press,
To a time of super computers, jet planes, and the rest.

This dramatic intellectual advance,
 Really did not happen simply by chance.
Their minds to problems great thinkers did apply,
To each problem, they had to know the reason why.
One answer usually led to another
As a result today we are all together.

This world has become a much smaller place,
There is no longer separation of people by race.
What was once the land of the Native Americans,
Is now home to Europeans, Asians and Africans.
Tremendous change this world has seen,
Never will it be the same again.

The twentieth century has brought
Scientific and technological changes,
Which new problems have wrought.
Time and History have certainly shown,
That greed for power has certainly grown.
One answer our great thinkers have failed to give,
How at peace the world may live.

The great challenge of the 21st century,
Is how to remove tensions and conflicts, and let peace be.
The number one problem of the present Age,
Is how to handle the power craze.
Man today who plans to conquer space,
Does not know how to live as part of the human race.

Until each life is given equal worth,
There will be no peace on this planet-Earth.
What is legal is not necessarily just,
In justice then, we should put our trust.
If there is no justice, there will be no peace,
Without peace, life as we know it shall certainly cease.

This book dear reader, I hope you will read,
In a new direction, others you might lead;
It is only by beginning today to care,
That this responsibility we will begin to share.
A step in the right direction this world will make,
When together we work for peace sweet sake.

THE AGE OF EXPLORATION AND THE COMING OF THE EUROPEANS

The Age Of Exploration

The Renaissance, or rebirth of learning, began during the 14th century. It brought to an end a period of about 1,000 years, during which tradition dominated European thinking. It began in response to a new interest in the achievements of classical Greece and Rome; the writings of Arab scholars, and knowledge obtained from travelers, about eastern cultures. It brought to an end, the Middle Age and introduced the Modern Age.

Throughout the Middle Ages, Europeans saw themselves as people of Christendom. With the coming of the Renaissance, the idea of the nation state was born. No longer was Latin the only language of importance. People began to value their own forms of speech and to write in their own languages.

The power of tradition was replaced by a new interest in science. Concepts about the universe, solar system and the world were changing. The belief in a round earth began to grow. A new spirit of exploration and adventure replaced fear of the seas. Navigational instruments recently invented, made sailors more confident and courageous.

Prince Henry the Navigator

Henry was a Portuguese prince. He was called the "Navigator" because of his interest in navigation. He was born in 1394 and died in 1460. He was a true "Renaissance man."

He established a school of Navigation at Sagres, in Southern Portugal. He gathered together mapmakers, geographers, mathematicians and sailors to explore the African coastline.

He hoped to:
- a) reach the source from which North Africans obtained gold for many centuries. b) establish relations with Prester John, the fabled Christian king in East Africa.
- c) cut off the supply of gold to North Africa.
- d) destroy the power of the Muslims in North Africa.
- e) spread Christianity.
- f) pioneer a sea route to the Far East.

By the time Prince Henry died in 1460, the Portuguese had explored the West African coast as far South as Sierra Leone. The first Africans were taken to Europe (Portugal) to be enslaved (1441). Contact was made with the gold producing region of West Africa, and the future of Portuguese voyages of exploration was assured.

From this point on, contact between Europe and West Africa would be maintained Fifty years later; the Americas would be brought into this intercontinental operation as a result of the successful westward voyages of Christopher Columbus.

Portugal continued the exploration of the African coastline. In 1488, Bartholomew Diaz rounded the Cape of Good Hope. In 1498, Vasco da Gama sailed directly from Portugal to India.

Prince Henry—The Navigator

In 1394 a Prince was born,
Interest in politics he certainly had none.
The Renaissance era had just begun,
Henry was destined to be a famous man.
Great things the Portuguese Prince hoped to achieve,
Before the breath, his body should leave.

The age of the Crusaders he certainly admired,
A plan for life the Crusaders inspired.
Prester John of East Africa he hoped to find,
John was a man of his own kind.
Working together Henry thought they should,
Muslims from North Africa, expel as early as they could.

The Christian message to Africa he hoped to bring,
African people to relieve of their sins.
His Christian expeditions had further dividends to pay,
A sea route to the Spice Islands might begin this way.
Of his mission in life he certainly was convinced,
His stars predicted it! He believed ever since.

A School of Navigation Prince Henry did establish,
At the south western tip of Portugal, a place called Sagres.
To his school Prince Henry, scholars did invite,
Map makers, brave sailors, men of navigational insight.
Christians or Muslims, Gentiles or Jews,
The only test required was that they loved navigation too.

In 1431 Gil Eannes rounded Cape Bojador,
Thus was opened the navigational door.
In 1441 Goncalves captured some Africans,
Brought them to Portugal and made them Christians.
Instruments of colonization, without being aware,
They functioned as interpreters and Christian pioneers.

In 1441 African gold to Portugal was brought,
This was a prize desperately sought.
Some Africans were taken to be enslaved,

Their Christian principles the Portuguese did waive.
Exploration continued at a fairly good pace,
Portugal was alone in the navigational race.

Two special voyages Cadamosto did make,
Careful records of his observations this sailor did take.
Up the Gambia Cadamosto did sail,
His exploits he recorded in very great detail.
The Azores, Cape Verde and Madeira,
Soon became parts of the Portuguese empire.

Fourteen sixty was the year of Henry's death,
His appointments in life he certainly met.
He did not find the Christian Prester John,
But fear of the sea certainly had gone.
The work he began was continued by the crown,
Never did they stop till Africa they sailed round.

In 1487 Diaz rounded the Cape,
The West coast of Africa was Portugal's to take.
In 1498 to India Da Gama did sail,
The Portuguese sailors certainly did not fail.
The journey to the Spice Islands was now a stone's throw,
Come on traders! To the islands we must go.

And so it was that an Empire was built,
On the dreams of a dreamer which he constantly felt.
Little Portugal on the edge of Iberia,
Was now to rule the Indies, India and Africa.
Gold, slaves, spices, and Indian luxury,
Were soon to become Portugal's monopoly.

The ways of life of people of the East,
Were soon to be condemned by the Portuguese.
Traditional religions of many Africans
Were soon attacked by Europeans Christians.
Chiefs, Elders and African Kings
Were soon to be enslaved by the Portuguese.

Europe In The Fifteenth Century Coming Out Of Darkness

The fall of Rome introduced a thousand years,
The Medieval Era is the title it bears.
European creativity certainly did stagnate,
It was the period when the Church came to dominate.
European life was thoroughly controlled—
By the dictates of the Church—which daily people were told.

Marco Polo's return from distant China
Evoked Europe's interest in gold and silver.
Two hundred years of war, called the Crusades,
Introduced Europe to Traditional Arab ways.
The Holy lands the Crusaders failed to win,
But the exchange of ideas certainly did begin.

By 1400 European isolation's end was near
Great men of ideas were born year after year.
Return to the greatness of Rome and Greece
And Medieval ideas will certainly cease.
It was out of such early circumstance
Came the exciting European Renaissance.

Remains of Greek and Roman architecture
Inspired many a creative European thinkers.
Curiosity about the natural environment
Caused many early scientist to decent—
From the guidelines the Church did lay
For Europeans to practice each and every day.

Their goal European thinkers were determined to achieve,
Foreign ideas they were willing to receive.
Ptolemy of Egypt had written of a round earth,
This idea proved to be of very great worth.
The Chinese, gunpowder early did make,
For amusement when festivals they did celebrate.

Records of Greek and Roman wisdom
Returned to enlighten modern Europeans.
The Portuguese copied the Arab's lateen sail
And totally redesigned their new caravel.
Thus European ships were re-designed
To undertake historic voyages of modern mankind.

The invention of the compass, quadrant, and astrolabe,
Revolutionized navigation in many ways.
With a new desire this world to explore
Nothing would stop them, there were barriers no more.
European scholars no longer thought it a sin
The mysteries of nature, investigation to begin.

The Overland Trade

For centuries on the Far East, Europe did depend
For goods which they needed but could not locally find.
Nutmegs, cloves and peppers too,
Were spices without which they could not do.
Luxury goods from the East traders brought
Such were the things the nobility eagerly sought.

Contact with the East was annually maintained,
By what was called the "overland trade".
Merchants and traders feared to travel by sea,
That was the place monsters were supposed to be.
The overland trade the Italians had won
Because of their position in the Mediterranean.

From Genoa, Florence and the city of Venice,
Eastern goods were shipped with Italian relish.
A crisis developed in 1453,
Overland trade was no longer to be.
Constantinople was captured by Ottoman Turks,
No longer would the system efficiently work.

A new way to the East the traders had to find,
This question occupied the European mind.
A route by sea Europeans had refused to consider,
Some were afraid of the great sea monsters.
The color of their skin certainly would turn black,
If the equator they crossed on their way back.

By myths and traditions for centuries they lived,
'Guidance for life' was the Church to give.
Their enjoyment of spice in former years
Led to a break with traditional ways.
As necessity is the mother of invention
Necessity led also to the Age of Navigation.

What began as a search for spice,
Would later result in European paradise.
European exploration once begun,
Would later result in empires they easily won.
European expansion would change the world,
Read on, Dear Reader, watch the story unfold.

CHAPTER-2

Exploration, Colonization and the African Presence in the Americas

<u>Renaissance</u>—One of the great changes brought about in Europe by the Renaissance was man's new awareness of himself and the world around him. It was this that led to the 'Age of Exploration.'

<u>Age of Exploration</u>—The Age of Exploration was that period in European history when people ventured out from Europe for the first time to make contact with far-away lands.

It began with the Portuguese. Prince Henry the Navigator, established a school at Sagres in Southern Portugal. This was to be the heart of his navigational program. He aimed at finding a route to the Spice Islands (East Indies) someday, by sailing around Africa.

Prince Henry died in 1460, the year that Portuguese sailors reached Sierra Leon. The program continued after his death and in 1498 Vasco da Gama sailed directly to India.

The Portuguese and Africa

Prince Henry's sailors began to explore the West African coastline in 1419.

By 1434, Gil Eannes reached Cape Bajador.

In 1441, the first group of Africans were taken out of Africa and brought to Portugal, given a Christian education and trained as interpreters.

In 1443, gold was brought back from West Africa to Portugal.

In 1488, Bartholomew Dias rounded the Cape of Good Hope.

In 1498, Vasco da Gama sailed directly from Portugal to India.

Some Effects of Portugal's Contact with Africa

1. Portugal gained knowledge about West Africa.

2. By taking Africans to Portugal to be trained in Christianity and as interpreters, Portugal introduced European culture into West Africa.

3. Portugal became aware of the rich gold mines of West Africa.

4. Portugal became aware of the trading possibilities in goods and African people.

5. By the 1440s, trade with West Africa had begun. In 1448, Portuguese merchants brought back gold dust, ostrich feathers, gum and Africans to be enslaved.

6. Between 1470 and 1475, Portuguese merchants brought back pepper, ivory and many Africans to be enslaved.

7. In 1481, the Portuguese King declared a Royal monopoly over the West African trade. The right to trade in Guinea (West Africa) was granted to syndicates who paid rent in "cash or slaves." <u>W. D. Hussey</u>

"The most valuable commodities traded were pepper, ivory, gold and slaves." <u>W. D. Hussey</u>

By the 1570s, the Portuguese established control over Angola which became the major supplier of Africans to be enslaved in Brazil.

The Portuguese, Arabs, and the Great West African Empires

The arrival of the Portuguese in West Africa produced competition against the Arabs in the Sudan.

Portuguese power was well established in the Sudan even before the fall of Mali. In its time of troubles, the King of Mali (Muslim) appealed to the Portuguese (Catholics) for help. Mali failed to get Portugal's help because of religious reasons.

Portugal's power grew during the period of the Songhai Empire. In 1591, the kingdom of Songhai was defeated by the Moroccans. This defeat had far reaching effects.

Results of the Fall of Songhai

1. The highly centralized system of government built up over a thousand years finally ended.

2. The Trans-Saharan trade, which was controlled by North African traders, (Muslims) was destroyed.

3. The people of the Sudan were left defenseless.

4. Portugal had a free hand to exploit West Africa.

5. The Arabs, having lost control of the <u>legitimate</u> trade in West Africa, concentrated more on the export of African people across the desert.

It was not long before the Portuguese arrived in East Africa, defeated the Arabs, established themselves and took over the trade to the Far East. Gold, ivory and African people to be enslaved, became the major sources of Portuguese wealth.

This East African trade, which was started by the Arabs and continued under the Portuguese, was responsible for the scattering of African people to places as far away as India, China and the East Indies.

The Spanish Empire in the West

<u>Treaty of Tordesillas</u>—For over 70 years, the Portuguese had been trying to reach the Far East by sailing around Africa. In an attempt to reach the Far East, Columbus, sailing for Portugal's rival ~ <u>Spain,</u> sailed westward. In less than 10 weeks, he reached an island in the Bahamas chain.

After his return to Spain, news of his success spread like wild fire. The Portuguese were alarmed. They reasoned that Columbus might have reached lands which were "rightfully" theirs. To settle this dispute, the matter was brought before the Pope. The Spanish and Portuguese finally agreed to a dividing line (Line of Demarcation), drawn 370 leagues west of the Azores. Spain got all of the Americas, except the extreme eastern tip of South America. This Agreement came to be called the Treaty of Tordesillas.

<u>Spain in the Caribbean</u>—The first Spanish colony was established on Hispaniola (Haiti). Among the plants brought to Haiti, was sugarcane.

Jamaica, Puerto Rico and Cuba were settled from Haiti. Sugar production soon proved to be an economic success.

Plantations were established. The Arawaks were the first source of labor then Africans were used.

The first Africans arrived in 1502 by way of Spain.

The first Africans to arrive by way of the Middle Passage arrived in 1518.

Africans became the source of labor in mines and on plantations in the islands of the Greater Antilles (West Indies).

Spanish exploration continued. By 1521, Spain controlled Mexico; by 1535, she controlled Peru. Interest in these gold-producing areas caused Spain to neglect the Caribbean.

Challenge to Spain's Power

Spain dominated the Americas for the entire 16ᵗʰ Century. With the opening of the new century, the tide began to turn. As a result of jealousy, the birth of Protestantism, Spain's use of her new found wealth to finance war-fare, and information about the inexhaustible amount of gold and silver in the Americas, other nations began to challenge Spain's power. Those challenges soon led to the establishment of colonies, which depended on the enslavement of Africans as a labor source.

The following is a list of some colonies settled by other nations:
1. The Virginia Colony (North America)—1607—British

2. St. Kitts (Caribbean)—1624—British and French

3. Barbados (Caribbean)—1630—British

4. Martinique and Guadeloupe—1635—French

5. Bahamas (Caribbean)—1648—British

6. Haiti (Caribbean)—1654—French

7. Jamaica (Caribbean)—1655—British

With the exception of Bahamas, all colonies in the Caribbean became major producers of sugar. Sugar plantations of the British, Spanish and French all depended on labor supplied by enslaved Africans. Sugar plantations in Brazil were also worked by Africans brought across the Middle Passage from Angola and other Portuguese controlled places in Africa.

North America

In North America, more and more, colonies were founded through the 17th century. At first, colonies in the South produced tobacco, indigo and rice. Later, cotton dominated the southern economy.

As was the case in the Caribbean, it was at the expense of Africa that the plantation system in the South (USA) developed.

Later Migration of African People

As a result of Lord Mansfield's decision in England in 1772, over 14,000 Africans were freed. Of this number, several hundred returned to Africa and settled in Sierra Leone.

Between 1783 and 1789, over 8,000 Loyalists and their slaves left the newly formed USA to settle in the Bahamas.

After the civil war, Liberia was founded to settle newly freed African Americans.

A group of African Americans left the USA to settle in Haiti in the latter part of the 19th Century.

Migration of Caribbean People

Slavery ended in the English-speaking Caribbean in 1838. Haiti won its independence 34 years earlier in 1804. By 1850, a massive movement of people began, from the islands to mainland America.

After the ending of slavery there was a massive movement of people from the Caribbean to Central America. Over 40,000 people moved from Jamaica alone to Honduras, Costa Rica and Panama. Most migrated in search of employment on the Panama Canal.

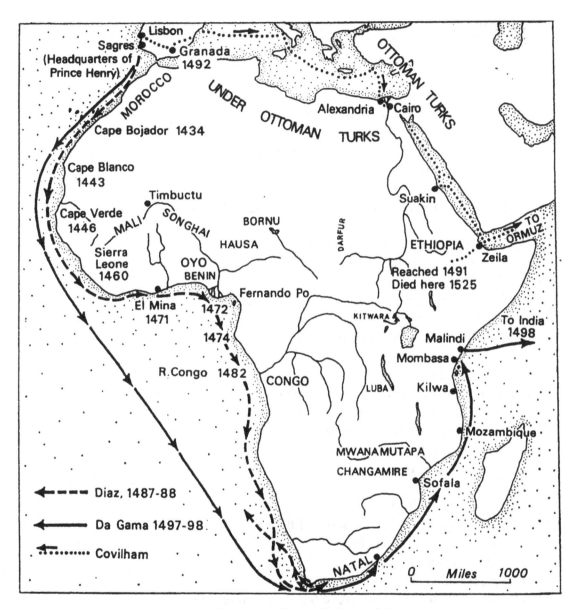

Portuguese Exploration of the African coast

Westward Oh!
Christopher Columbus Pursues His Dreams

Europe was concerned about Portugal's possible success.
Portugal's monopoly would hurt all the rest.
Though they were worried—what could they do?
The ways to the East were but a few.
There were some who believed that the world was round,
But they did not believe a Westward route could be found.

It was Christopher Columbus, a Genoese,
Who trusted his life to the Westward breeze.
As a child, many stories Columbus did hear
About land and people across the sea somewhere.
To Portugal and France Columbus did appeal
For assistance to find if these stories were real.

Portugal, France and England too
Refused to help him! He knew not what to do.
To Spain this Italian finally did turn,
His dream within, continued to burn.
The Spanish monarchs liked his plan,
"We promise to help as soon as we can."

For eight long years this pioneer did wait,
Before the Atlantic expedition got out of the gate.
The Pinta, Nina, Santa Maria too
Were soon completely out of view.
Spain's support for this risky expedition
Was the result of the desire to spread the Christian religion.

Wealth and power had their place
 In Spain's decision to join this race.
A route to the East, Columbus had hoped to find.
This thought was daily on his mind.
He left Palos on August three,
The first to the Spice Islands he hoped to be.

Southward to the Canaries this explorer did sail,
Leaving behind him a good luck trail.
Westward into the Atlantic sailed the fleet,
Determined to find the land of spices sweet.
October 12 was a very special day,
Their efforts were rewarded in a very special way.

There in the distance an island stood,
Covered with pines and cedar wood.
Spain's flag and Cross in the sand Columbus planted,
Soon he was asking for things Spain wanted.
"Gold and silver, the things you seek,
Can be found to the South". So said the Cacique.

The Spaniards were treated like honored guests,
By these friendly Indians of the west.
Columbus sailed South from San Salvador,
Gifts of gold he wanted some more.
"Go to the East" the Indians of Cuba directed,
Columbus did and became ship wrecked.

The Indians of Haiti Columbus's possessions saved
From the wrecked vessel beneath the Tropical waves.
On the island of Haiti a Spanish fort was built,
All along Columbus was suffering guilt.
Indian friendship, love and hospitality,
He planned one day to reward with slavery.

Back to Spain Columbus prepared to go,
His plan for the future only he knew.
Thirty eight men he left behind
To hold the land for Isabella and her kind.
Six Indians he took back to Spain with him
As proof of the land to which he had been.

A great hero in Spain, Columbus was hailed
Across the Atlantic this dreamer had sailed.
He was graciously received at the Spanish court
The Monarchs realized what his voyage was worth.
New lands to spread Christianity!
There too untold treasures might be.

Three more voyages this dreamer undertook
Spanish settlers to the New World. each time he took.
Fame and fortune each Spaniard hoped to gain;
As the months passed such dreams began to wane.

Columbus soon lost his national prestige
And later died Admiral of the Ocean Seas.

Between fourteen ninety four and fifteen o' four
The entire Caribbean this man did explore.
He cruised the coast of the American mainland,
Still in search of the coveted Spice Islands.
To Spain he gave wealth and untold power,
To the Indians, a miserable, dismal future.

His story is a lesson in what you can achieve,
When in your dreams you continue to believe.
On that August morn when he sailed out into the blue,
Columbus did not realize what that simple act would do.
Lest I forget, let me say it now that I can,
One of his sea captains was an <u>African.</u>

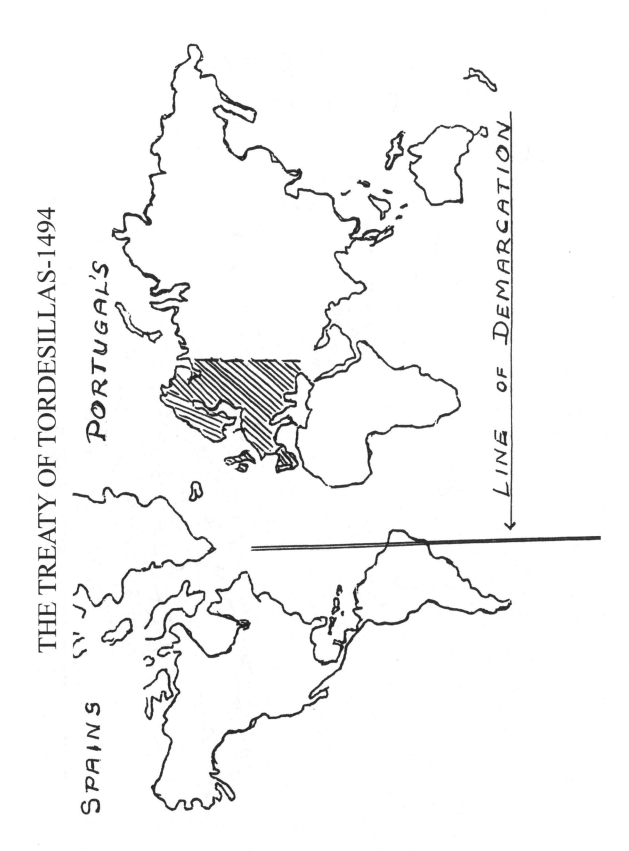

THE TREATY OF TORDESILLAS-1494

PORTUGAL'S

LINE OF DEMARCATION

SPAINS

LATIN AMERICA
THE TREATY OF TORDESILLAS

1   Mexico

Central America:

2 Guatemala
3 Honduras
4 El Salvador
5 NNicaragua
6 Costa Rica
7 Panama

Caribbean:

  8   Cuba
  9   Dominican Republic
10   Puerto Rico

South: America:

11   . Venezuela
12   Colombia
13   Ecuador
14   Peru
15   Bolivia
16   Paraguay
17   Chile
18   Argentina
19   Uruguay

Let There Be Peace!
The Treaty Of Tordesillas

Columbus' success caused Portugal much pain,
"For over sixty years we have tried—now it's all in vain".
This was what the Portuguese thought,
Since it seemed Columbus had arrived in the land they sought.
In 1492 Columbus landed on a Bahamian beach,
Portuguese sailors, India still did not reach.

"Ours is the land the Spaniards have claimed,
We will stand up for our rights! We will not be defamed"
This was the position of Portugal,
Ready to defend her nationals.
With Portugal's position Spain could not agree,
She had provided Columbus' ships which numbered three.

Christianity to the Indians Isabella was determined to bring,
Souls to save was her 'major thing'.
Ferdinand of Spain was no pious king,
To him, wealth and power had a much better ring.
Spain and Portugal came face to face,
To settle the early beginnings of the colonial race.

The Pope of Rome had to be a diplomat,
He could not offend either! Remember that.
The map of the world he did divide,
Lands to the East was on Portugal's side
West of the line fell to the country—
Spain, Soon to exploit the Spanish main.

So dear reader, now you understand,
How the Spaniards came to own these valuable lands.
To Portugal was given the Spice Islands—
India, Madeira and African lands.
The entire America, Spain could settle at will,
All except the Eastern tip of the giant Brazil.

Thus it was that the world was shared,
Between two little nations as if no other cared.
The Pope had unwittingly set the stage,
For European nations, wars to wage.
The Pope's dictates no one did contradict,
As long as Europe remained purely Catholic.

For a thousand years Europe, the Church did control
Few questioned the teachings! A place in heaven they worked to ensure.
The first challenge to the Pope came from within.
Luther raised the question of clerical sin.
This act of "faith" created a crisis,
No longer would there be unity among the Catholics.

Out of the Reformation new Churches were born,
The Papal monopoly certainly was gone.
The political repercussions were to no one's surprise,
International conflicts were soon to arise.
The French and Dutch and good old England,
Soon sailed westward to claim their share of the lands.

LATIN AMERICA AND THE CARIBBEAN

LATIN AMERICA

SPANISH SPEAKING COUNTRIES (LATIN, AMERICAN)

1. Mexico

Central America:
2. Guatemala
3. Honduras
4. El Salvador
5. Nicaragua
6. Costa Rica
7. Panama

Caribbean
8. Cuba
9. Dominican Republic
10. Puerto Rico

South America:
11. Venezuela
12. Colombia
13. Ecuador
14. Peru
15. Bolivia
16. Paraguay
17. Chile
18. Argentina
19. Uruguay

Introduction To The History And Cultures Of Latin America

In an attempt to reach the Far East by sailing westward, Columbus accidentally reached San Salvador, Bahamas on October 12, 1492.

He sailed southward, stopped at Cuba, then on to Haiti where he was ship-wrecked.

He built the first Spanish out-post in the New World, named it Port Navidad and sailed back to Spain.

News of his success led to conflict with Portugal which had been attempting to reach the Far East for many years. A dispute over land developed between Spain and Portugal.

The dispute was settled by the Treaty of Tordisillas which gave Spain the New World, with the exception of the extreme eastern tip of Brazil.

Columbus made three more voyages during which he explored the entire Caribbean and the coast of Central America.

Columbus was appointed first governor of Hispaniola.

In 1503 Nicholas Ovando became governor.

In 1509 Columbus' son Diego was made governor.

While Diego was governor Puerto Rico, Jamaica, and Cuba were settled.

Development of mines and plantations on the Caribbean islands, led to the destruction of the Arawaks (original inhabitants)

Africans were brought in to provide labor for the mines and plantations.

Hernando Cortez, secretary to the governor of Cuba sailed to Mexico in 1519.

By 1521 the Aztec Empire was conquered.

Mexico was rich in gold and Spain turned its attention to the exploitation of Mexican resources, gold and silver.

It took Spain a long time, however, the great Inca Empire was overthrown and Spain controlled another gold rich region.

Old Peru extended over the western half of South America.

News of Spain's wealth from the New World led to challenges from other European nations—the British, French, Dutch.

Spain established a highly centralized form of government over her empire. Decisions pertaining to the government of the Spanish Empire were made by the Council of the Indies, over which the Spanish King had the right to preside.

The Council of the Indies appointed officials to reside in and rule over the empire.

The leading officials were the Viceroys, Members of the Audiencas, Governor and Members of the Cabildos.

All positions except those at the lowest level were given to Penisulares. This was to ensure loyalty to Spain.

Creoles were seen as a threat and were not trusted with important positions.

Creoles—those born in the colonies, were angry at the way they were treated by Spain. When (at the time of the Napoleonic Wars) the Creoles saw their chance, they revolted and declared their independence from Spain.

THE SPANISH EMPIRE

| | | Officials |
| | 2 | 2 | Council of Lawyers |

Officials

Council of Lawyers

Governor

Town Council

Viceroy

Structure of the Government of the Spanish Empire

Key 1 Viceroyalty
2 Audencia
3 Province
4 Cabildo

An End And A Beginning

In 1517 an event took place
Which would later change the colonial race.
Martin Luther questioned the Church and Pope,
This sowed seeds of a feeling of hope.
Soon Calvin and Zwingli did break away,

It was not long before it as Old England's day.
New doctrines the Protestants began to teach,
The salvation of his soul was the business of each.
The way to heaven was of great variety,
This was the result of Protestant Christianity.
A thousand years of control finally did end,
European nations their rights they did defend.

Martin Luther's questions fractured Christian unity,
And weakened the power of the traditional Papacy.
The Papal Treaty of 1494,
Commanded the respect of Europe no more.
Catholic Spain, its Empire had to defend,
Protestant nations on America did descend.

Privateers, buccaneers and pirates too,
Sailed the water of the Caribbean blue—'
Gold and silver these sea rovers did rob,
Their rulers commended—"You have done a good job."
Thus it was that the challenge began,
Spain would lose her possessions, one by one.

Britain, Holland and the country France
Had now joined in the exciting colonial dance.
Raleigh, Holland and Sir Humphrey Gilbert,
Expounded the doctrines of colonial worth.
Sir Walter Raleigh was a major colonizer,
He played a part in founding Guiana.

Thomas Warner founded a colony on St. Kitts
Soon to be followed by Antigua, Montserrat and little Nevis.
Soon from Virginia these colonies did learn,
From tobacco cultivation, a living they could earn,
Caribbean colonies Virginia did undersell,
Caribbean economies stopped doing very well.

With the coming of sugar a new age began.
This came to be called The Sugar Revolution
The Caribbean economies sugar did change,
The quiet little islands would never be the same again.
Sugar created an insatiable demand
For slaves to work at European command.

The slave trade from Africa which the Portuguese began
Was soon to be joined by many other lands.
The British and Dutch, French and Swedes
Joined in the trade of defenseless human beings.
For over three centuries the Atlantic was crossed,
Europe's gains were Africa's loss.

Millions and millions of Africa's best,
Crossed the Atlantic to fill the planter's chests.
Fathers and mothers and children too,
Came to America to begin life anew.
Roles and positions, status and class
All had to be relinquished—they were things of the past.

CHAPTER-3

ANCIENT & TRADITIONAL AFRICA

Egypt
Where Our Story Begins

Egypt is sometimes described as the gift of the Nile. This is a very fitting description. Without the Nile there would be no Egypt.

The River Nile flows from the mountains in the South, northward to the eastern Mediterranean. It flows northward for over 4000 miles, converting what would otherwise be a sandy waste into highly productive farmlands.

Throughout history the annual flooding of the Nile enriched the lands of the valley through which the river flows. The annual supply of silt brought down by the river is the key to an understanding of the development of the earliest communities in the Nile Valley.

A Search for Knowledge

Jimmy

Grandpa! Grandpa!
Please answer this one if you can,
It is a question about Africa's 'early man'!
Please answer my question, I really want to know
How the earliest community began to grow?
How the first seeds did man decide to sow?
How the answers to "questions" people got to know?
How from a wandering food seeking band,
People settled and began to develop the land?
How without modern scientific education,
Egypt became the world's first great civilization?

Grandpa

Jimmy my boy—this is a very difficult one,
However, I will do for you the best that I can.
Let us imagine that I was a part
Of the earliest civilization from the start.

Let us go back thousands of years to the time of the birth of the earliest communities. Let us try to understand how it might have happened. Day after day before people lived in settled communities, people and animals went down to the river to drink.

Soon we noticed that animals usually gather at certain places by the river. Such places soon became favorite hunting grounds. The richness of the alluvial soil brought down by the river resulted in the prolific growth of plants including edible plants in the river valley. We soon realized that hunting and gathering could be done at the same place. Thus, the availability of a supply of good clean water, the abundance of animals frequenting the area (to drink) and the easy reach of edible plants and fruits provided reason enough for us to limit our wandering.

And then it happened! It was discovered that it was not necessary for plants to grow naturally as conditions of the environment allowed. We realized that the seeds could be planted; growing plants could be cared for and abundant harvests would result. This was the way agriculture began.

The planting, tending and harvesting of crops led to the beginning of a settled life. Thus, the earliest communities were born. Domestication of plants soon led to the domestication of animals and so an entirely new way of life developed.

As time passed, communities grew in size. With the growth in size of communities conflicts developed. In an attempt to limit the number of conflicts, rules (laws) became necessary. All members of a community were soon expected to know the rules (laws) and to obey them. Failure to obey the (rules) laws led to consequences; and so a system of justice evolved.

With experience, agricultural production became more and more efficient. More food could be produced with fewer workers. Displaced workers found employment in other areas as the growing complexity of society created new demands and therefore further division of labor or specialization.

Not only was there improvement in the quantity and quality of products, there was also improvement in the organization and operation of society.

New opportunities were created for leaders at every level. Soon there were skilled professionals such as doctors, judges, craftsmen, architects, and scholars; all, the products of the demands of society.

There were writers, record keepers, and men of ideas. In addition, there arose a special group whose function it was to be concerned with life after death. There were others too, whose major concern was to understand nature—the planetary system, the seasons, the sun, the moon and the world around us. It was not long before the questions—"Who are we"? "Why are we here?—arose.

Such profound questions about humanity and the world, led to a search for an explanation. Thus began the concept of a Supreme Being. As time passed a priestly cast evolved. Their major concern being not only the good life on earth, but also life after death.

Later the society produced a leader in whose person were linked the responsibility for matters pertaining to daily living (political) and matters pertaining to life after death (spiritual). He was the personification of the beliefs, aspirations, and dreams of the Egyptian people. He was the Pharaoh. The Pharaoh was soon to be seen as a god. He was all-powerful.

From its early beginning as a simple farming community, Egypt grew from strength to strength. As time passed she was faced with numerous challenges; challenges which led to increased complexity and achievements. Egyptian ingenuity and creativity in coping with her perennial challenges led to the development of one of the greatest civilizations the world has known.

Egypt distinguished herself in many areas of life, and has contributed much to Western Civilization. Mathematics, astronomy, architecture, art, literature, medicine are but a few of the areas in which the Egyptian civilization has contributed to the development of Western Civilization. Scholars today still marvel at the accomplishments of the Egyptians.

After more than 5000 years of growth, inventions, innovation, progress and unprecedented accomplishments, the Egyptian civilization peaked and began to decline.

Its decline was hastened by a series of invasions and conquests. It all began with a period of extended warfare between Egypt and Kush. Eventually Kush was defeated by Egypt. A very long period of cultural exchange followed; so much so, that there was little difference between the two kingdoms ~ culturally. Egypt however, continued to weaken and was invaded and defeated by Kush. The close relationship between Egypt and Kush continued until the combined powers were defeated by an invasion from Assyria.

Some historians argue that the Assyrians were victorious because of superior weaponry; the invading Assyrians fought with weapons made of metal, while the Kushite/Egyptian forces did not. It was this defeat which stimulated the development of Meroe's metal industry. The large deposit of iron ore and the availability of wood for fuel made it quite easy to mine and smelt iron at Meroe. Iron production led to the development of an industry for the production of weapons and agricultural implements.

Meroe's new position of power soon led to conquest and expansion into neighboring lands. Industrial development led naturally to an expansion of commercial activities. Soon, the influence of the Nile Valley could be felt from the Central African region, to West Africa and the Mediterranean region. Ideas which originated in Egypt would now find their way through North, East, Central and West Africa. Taking into consideration the pattern of the early trade routes, there was far greater possibility for the spread of ideas than was assumed by historians until modern times.

Egypt was later invaded by Greece. This invasion which was followed by conquest led to further cultural exchange. Much that was Egyptian found its way into Europe by way of Greece and Greek ideas also blended into Egyptian culture. Christianity soon spread from Egypt southward into Nubia by the Greeks and Egyptians.

European influence introduced by Greece was soon to be strengthened by the Roman conquerors. Soon North African peoples were exposed to elements of the cultures of people of South Europe (Greeks and Romans); they were also to be influenced by Egypt and cultures of the upper Nile.

The rise of Islam in the 7th century had the most far-reaching effect on the Egyptian way of life; and the way of life of the entire North African region. With the coming of Islam, Egypt and the entire North African region experienced far reaching cultural changes; Islam being not just a new religion, but an entirely new way of life.

For many centuries earlier, North African peoples conducted a very important trade across the Sahara with the people of West Africa. After the arrival of Islam, not only would traders be taking trade goods across the Sahara, they would take a new religion and cultural ideas as well.

The impact of Islam was first to be felt in Ghana, the first of the Great West African Empires, and later to a greater extent in Mali and Songhai.

AFRICA! OH AFRICA!

Africa! Oh Africa! Birthplace of humanity,
Africa!, Dear Africa! Land of much controversy.
Good Mother that thou art, you have given from your heart
Your wisdom and children; you've played your part.

The greatness of Egypt, some have tried to deny,
Though this is impossible, they continue to try.
Science and art are among your contributions,
To the things you've given to Western civilization.

Africa! Oh Africa! What's in a name!
Your true place in History 'tis time to reclaim.
Your children have awakened joyfully at last,
To make known to the world, the truth of your past.

Africa! Oh Africa! Land of variety
Of climate and animals everywhere you see.
Mountains and deserts your borders do embrace,
Grassland and forest each in its place.

Africa! Oh Africa! Great
Empires you once had,
Memories of which, make the heart glad.
Ghana, Songhai and ancient Mali
Were centers of trade, and much industry.

Africa! Oh Africa! These are some names
Of men of distinction, of men of great fame.
Mansa Musa of Mali, great Emperor was he,
Great warrior/state builder was Sonni Ali.

Askia the Great was a very special man,
For his state, Songhai, he had a good plan.
At Gao, Walata and Timbuktu,
He built universities, not just for a few.

43

From Europe and Asia many scholars did come,
To obtain knowledge they had not at home.
Africa! Dear Africa! Be of good cheer!
The truth of your past will be taught again.

Africa! Dear Africa! Don't indulge your pain.
Africa, Oh Africa! Africa, Dear Africa!
You shall be great again.
Yes! You shall be great again.

THE GOLDEN AGE
OF
WEST AFRICA

Great West African Empires

Worldwide, the stories of Africa that appeared,
Were designed to evoke distrust and fear.
Stories of monsters, savages and sub-human,
Creating a totally false Western impression.

The colonizers their purpose successfully achieved,
The worst about Africa, they got people to believe.
Exploitation of the continent was easier justified,
When in colonizers the truth appeared to abide.

Books were written and many movies too,
To instill the colonizers' point of view.
Of the greatness of Mali and Ghana, nothing was said,
All that they read was propaganda instead.

Modern research can now refute,
European myths, peddled as truth:
Thousands of books are now available,
To destroy the myths and colonizers' fables.

The following poems as you will see,
Tell the story of Ghana, Songhai and Mali.
Success in administration, education and trade,
All three empires dramatically made.

Ancient Ghana (Land Of Gold)

The fascinating history of Ancient Ghana,
Began the Golden Age of West Africa.
As early as the year four hundred A.D.
Ghana embarked on prosperity.

Ghana's position on a route of trade
Foundations of an Empire successfully laid.
Traders from the North through the Empire did pass,
Tribute they paid in quantities vast.

Salt from the North was exchanged for gold,
Then in the North the gold was sold.
Ghana's wealth she did invest
In developing an army for future conquest.

Government was known for its efficiency,
This the result of a good bureaucracy.
Social services and housing were of the best,
Courts were established to ensure justice.

A new religion the traders brought with them,
It's name was Islam, otherwise called Muslim.
A new city they were allowed to build,
The strangers could do whatever they willed.

Ghana embarked on a period of conquest,
Subduing its neighbors to the East and West.
It's imperial borders Ghana did over extend,
Subjugation of others caused it to lose friends.

A crisis developed when the Almoravids
Attempted to do what Ghana did.
A revolt against Ghana began at last,
Subject peoples tried to recapture their past.

The Empire of Ghana gradually declined,
When financial resources it could not find.
A new power emerged quite gradually,
This was to be the Kingdom of Mali.

Kingdom Of Mali

About 1235 a new kingdom did begin,
The glory of Ghana it was destined to win.
Its economy, like Ghana's, was built on trade,
Agriculture its part efficiently played.
The river Niger played an important part,
Providing the kingdom's water transport.

Mohammed's religion, Mali's kings embraced,
Their subjects would follow at a very quick pace.
In 1324 a historic pilgrimage was made,
His respects to the Prophet, Mansa Musa paid.
From Mali to Egypt, then on to Mecca,
Mansa Musa traveled in very great splendor.

The story of this pilgrimage in Europe was told,
Especially the part about Mansa Musa's gold.
Accompanied by an entourage of eighty-thousand,
The king gave gold as he crossed the land.
The amount was such as you will see,
Its effect on Egypt was inflationary.

Scholars he brought on his return,
A thirst for knowledge within him did burn.
Schools he built—not just a few.
He established the University of Timbuktu.
Students arrived from far and near
Education to them was very dear.

From North Africa and the Islamic Middle East,
Professors arrived as knowledge increased.
Architects, judges and lawyers too,
Came to make of Mali a kingdom new.
A Muslim state Mali became,
Centuries to last like Mansa Musa's fame.

The teachings of Allah, Ghana did tolerate,
In Mali they became the principles of the state.
Government, justice and education,
Gained for Mali a worldwide reputation.
Thus through leadership and organization,
Mali became the new power of the Sudan.

Alas! The great Mansa Musa finally died,
Mali declined before the power of Songhai.
Competition for wealth and religious conflicts too,
Caused the decline of kingdom number two.
In place of the great kingdom of Mali,
Rose Songhai ruled by the warrior Sunni Ali.

More about Mali, history lovers should read,
Read about its leaders' extraordinary deeds.
Read of Sundiata's wisdom, courage and ability,
Read how he gained his vassal's loyalty.
Read how he conquered ancient Ghana
And the gold producing land of Wangara.

The Kingdom Of Songhai

The people of Songhai had a fascinating history,
Dating as far back as the middle of the ninth century.
Agriculture, fishing and the cattle industry,
Became the basis of Songhai's early economy.
Much wealth the early citizens did make,
Songhai became a very prosperous state.

Gao, the spiritual centre of Songhai,
The power of Mali it would soon defy.
In thirteen seventy five it broke away,
Growing in wealth and power day after day.
In fourteen sixty four it's fortune took a turn,
Of Sonni's reign we now will learn.

Like Sundiata, of the kingdom of Mali,
Was the king of Songhai, Sonni Ali.
Warrior, liberator and administrator was he,
No one dared defy his authority.
His entire reign, he devoted to affairs of state,
Matters of religion he left to Askia the Great.

Askia gained power by way of a coup,
He deposed Sonni's son Abubakar Dao.
He used Islam as a unifying force,
On his pilgrimage to Mecca forever he could boast.
On his return from Mecca, Askia brought,
Architects and scholars and advisors of all sorts.

The Imperial Government was thoroughly modernized,
In spite of the Empire's enormous size.
International trade continued to be
An important part of Songhai's economy.
Gold and ivory were major exports,
Salt and horses were important imports.

Institutions of learning were among Askia's priority,
Chief among these was the University of Sankore.
Scholars and professors from far and near,
Arrived at Sankore their wisdom to share.
Sankore was on par with Europe's best,
Oxford, Cordoba, Paris and the rest.

Thus it was by fifteen thirty,
Songhai had achieved great prosperity.
Songhai was the last player on West Africa's stage,
It closed the last chapter of The Golden Age.
It's last great rulers were Sonni Ali,
And Askia The Great, or Muhammed Toure.

Political conflicts introduced a period of decline,
Askia could do nothing, he was infirm and blind.
Songhai finally received a severe death blow,
It was invaded by forces from Morocco.
The Warriors fought courageously,
But were no match for the Moroccan enemy.

The Moroccans employed thousands of mercenaries,
From Spain, Portugal and distant Turkey.
The decisive victory of Songhai's enemy
Was simply the result of superior technology.
Bow and arrows, clubs and spears,
Were no match for European Musketeers.

By sixteen hundred, West Africa's fortune had turned.
Gone was the glory which the region had earned.
A thousand years of continuous prosperity
Was brought to an end by the Moroccan military.
West Africa's history from the Seventeenth century
Would be controlled from the Gulf of Guinea.

Britain and France and the enterprising Dutch,
Were soon trading gold, slaves, ivory and such.
The economic fortunes of colonized America,
Were soon to depend on the misfortunes of Africa.
A people who for centuries were noble and great,
Were soon reduced to a very dismal state.

Slavery The Old Fashioned Way

The institution of slavery was very old,
When the first Africans to the New World were sold.
In Europe and Asia and America too,
Slaves were kept, various jobs to do.
Slavery in Africa was nothing new,
A man could be enslaved for payment overdue.
Prisoners of war did sometimes spend
Time in slavery. Their position they did comprehend.

Social misfits would sometimes spend time,
To repay society for their various crimes.
A man would himself sometimes sell,
If his family on hard times unfortunately fell.
At no time at all, in ancient history,
Was a slave regarded as a piece of property.
Each slave, his position in society knew,
To freedom he returned when he had paid his due.

The work of slaves would always vary
According to the needs of society.
Some served in fields, some served in homes,
Some served in Greece as well as in Rome.
Some were used to carry their masters' loads
Mile after mile along the dusty roads.
Some were important government officials,
They protected their masters from jealous rivals.

And so my reader as you will see,
That was a different kind of slavery.
A slave held a place that he could understand,
A man was a slave and a slave was a man.
A slave could be black, a slave could be white,
No part did color play in the master's sight.
Slavery was given a new definition,
On the distant New World slave plantation.

In the Americas dear reader, as you will see,
A slave was NOT a part of society.
With the mules and horses they were classified,
The laws of nature the masters defied.
The slaves they regarded as property,
Completely removed from the human family.
This situation was at the base,
Of today's problems based on race.

Good Bye Africa! Good Bye!

In spite of Las Casas' desperate appeal,
The Indians did not survive the plantation ordeal.
In an attempt to save them from destruction,
He recommended the use of Africans.
Thus by fifteen twenty the stage was set,
Workers from Africa's West were America's to get.

Thus, the slave trade from Africa began,
Spain had an agreement with Portugal.
The British soon demanded their rightful share,
Of Spanish laws they did not fear.
Adventurers like Hawkins and Francis Drake,
Realized the fortunes that Britain could make.

Year after year to the Caribbean they would go,
Trying desperately to gain the Asiento.
For years Spanish colonies the British did supply,
Slaves from Africa which they were willing to buy.
With the coming of cotton a new age began,
Bleak was the future of the Africans.

The people of Africa lived in fear,
Of leaving the land they loved so dear.
Kings and Princes and peasants too,
Dreaded the thought of some place new.
Some were captured and marched to the coast,
To meet situations which were even worse.

Teeth were checked and their bodies too,
Reasons for this the Africans did not know.
Their bodies were shaven—gone was their hair,
Such an experience increased their fear.
In the barracoons the African slaves daily would stay,
Until finally the ship arrived one terrible day.

Then from the barracoons to the ship,
Doing what they did at the lash of a whip.
Then when the ship was tightly packed,
Into the wind the vessel would tack.
Men and women without any clothes,
Lying defenselessly in so many rows.

Across the Atlantic the vessel would sail,
Following dutifully in the former's trail.
Conditions grew worse as the days did pass,
Many hadn't the strength the journey to last.
Cholera, dysentery, diarrhea too,
Killed many of the 'cargo' and also the crew.

Many did attempt to commit suicide,
That's how much they feared life on the other side.
Finally when land was drawing near,
They were taken on deck for a breath of fresh air.
Bodies were shaven, again, at this stage,
In an attempt to hide individuals' age.

When after many weeks had passed,
The dreaded Atlantic the vessel had crossed.
Finally when the vessel had safely docked,
Africans were put on the auction block.
Soon from the dock to the plantations they would go,
What there awaited them they did not know.

So it was, for over three hundred years,
Africans were brought, in spite of their tears.
Many who left never land did see,
Their spirits still cry out from the bottom of the sea.
Africa lost twenty million or more,
Before the closing of the traders' door.

Towards Colonial Control

A thousand years the 'Golden Age' had been,
About the time Europe's Dark Ages had seen.
In Africa ten centuries of continuous progress,
In Europe, Civilization had certainly regressed.
Then as fate would have it, the tide did turn,
Reasons for this, you now will learn.

Out of the darkness Europe advanced,
As a result of the Renaissance.
Africa was experiencing internal change,
Of unprecedented scope and range.
With ships, guns, and ammunition,
Europe began its 'Age of Exploration'

Soon the gold mines were in Portugal's hands,
Key individuals were made Christians.
Africa to Portugal the Pope had granted,
She had the right to take what she wanted
The stage for the future now was set,
Portugal's new fortunes were Africa's regrets.

Portugal's newly found Eastern Empire,
Was soon to come under European fire
The Dutch were the first, their interest to show,
Soon colonial seeds had begun to grow.
The British and French were to follow soon
They built massive forts and the dreaded barracoons.

Soon Africa became part of the colonial system,
Entwined in the web of Mercantilism,
And so it was, that it all began,
The control of Africa and the Africans.
Once begun, there was no turning back,
No way to reverse the hands of the clock.

With the nineteenth century a new plan began,
It was a move towards emancipation.
In 1807 the slave trade came to an end,
No more on the Indies did Britain depend
New interest in Africa Europeans began to show
Missionaries, and explorers to Africa did go.

Colonization, commerce and Christianity,
Were now to be the road to prosperity.
The opposite was the case as you will see,
Africa was to lose its liberty.
The Europeans had come this time to stay,
They aimed to change the traditional way.
Africa came under European control,
Gone were its land, its diamond and gold.
Unofficial spheres of influence
Were later assigned at the Berlin Conference.
Europe soon controlled the entire Africa.
Except Liberia and ancient Ethiopia.

African problems would be easily understood,
If people would do what they daily should.
Read of Europe's arrival from the earliest date,
Read about the beginnings of the modern states.
Read about Cecil Rhodes and gold rich Rhodesia,
And the Dutch Reform Church of South Africa.

Read the story of Lord Lugard and Nigeria,
And the Mau Mau wars of early Kenya.
Read of the French in Algeria,
And the confusing story of Somalia.
Whatever you read you'll soon detect,
That Africans were treated without respect.

Europe's desire was to exploit,
This was easy; Europe had the might.
African culture was thoroughly ignored.
Traditional cultures were respected no more.
A fascinating continent, greatly misunderstood,
Read its history, I think you should.

CHAPTER-4

SAILING WEST TO REACH THE EAST

The Caribbean Story

The First Caribbean People

About 2000 years ago two groups of people arrived in the Caribbean from South America. They were the Arawaks and the Caribs. The Arawak Indians, were the first to arrive. Their arrival was the result of a desperate attempt to escape from their war-like neighbors the Caribs.

Both groups were at a very early stage of development; when the first Europeans arrived. They lived in simple houses, built of wattle and thatch. They hunted and fished with simple tools made of wood, bone or stone. They grew cassava, corn and potatoes. They dressed in simple loincloth made of cotton, which they wove themselves.

The Arawaks believed in gods of various types. They worshipped the moon, the sun, and gods which they believed caused the winds and rain. In addition, the Arawaks worshipped images they called—Zemis.

Life among these people was simple. Most of their time was spent in search of food. With the exception of an occasional hurricane or Carib raid, the Arawaks had little to worry about. They believed that after death they all went to Coyaba—(heaven).

The Coming Of the First Europeans

On October 12, 1492, Christopher Columbus arrived off the coast of a little Bahamian island known today as San Salvador. His arrival changed the course of history.

What were the factors which led to this historic event? Europe had been passing through a period known as the Middle Ages for nearly a thousand years. This period was marked by a dominance of tradition and the control of the Catholic Church. However, there were changes taking place, which though gradual were having far reaching effects on events of the time. These changes were all part of a new European movement known as the Renaissance. Good examples of these changes were as follows:

Some people began to question traditional teachings, and to search for answers to questions which to them were of great concern. Others improved the design of ships by borrowing ideas from people such as the Arabs. Navigational instruments were invented and better maps drawn. Most importantly, thinkers began to question the traditional view of the shape of the earth and to think about the possibility of sailing the oceans. All these developments gave rise to what would later be called—The Age of Exploration.

The Age of Exploration

This is a term used to describe that period in European History when Europeans for the first time set out to sail the Oceans and establish contact with faraway lands. It began when a Portuguese Prince—Henry the Navigator decided to find a sea route around Africa to the Spice Islands in the east. He established a school of navigation at Sagres to which he invited geographers, mapmakers, and mathematicians. Step by step Prince Henry's sailors explored the African coast, reported on their observations and drew maps of the areas they visited.

The Portuguese were experiencing great success in their attempt to reach the far east, when another adventurer arrived on the European scene. His name—Christopher Columbus.

Christopher Columbus and the "Westward Voyage

Columbus was born in Genoa, Italy. At an early age he developed an interest in the sea. He first went to sea; sailing on a Portuguese merchant ship. More and more he became convinced that it was possible to sail westward to reach the Spice Islands in the east.

After failing to receive support from England, Portugal and France he turned to Spain. The Spanish monarchs provided him with ships, supplies and men. Columbus set out on his historic voyage on August 3, 1492 from Palos Harbor. On October 12, 1492, he landed at a little island in the Bahamas known to the local inhabitants as Guanahani.

Columbus was well received by the Lucayan Indians—(Arawaks). They gave him gifts, receiving in return gifts which Columbus and his men had brought from Spain. The adventurers noticed that the Arawaks adorned their bodies with pieces of gold. They asked where could the gold be found. The Arawaks directed them to sail southwards. Columbus re-named the island San Salvador and left in search of the island from which the Lucayans had obtained gold.

After sailing through the southern Bahamas, Columbus arrived off the northeastern coast of Cuba. He again asked for gold and was directed by the Arawaks on the island of Cuba to sail eastward. He was shipwrecked off the north-coast of Haiti. The Indians helped Columbus to salvage as much as they could from the wrecked ship. Columbus built a fort on Haiti (Hispaniola) and named it La Navidad. He left 38 men to hold the island for Spain and to search for gold. Columbus sailed back to Spain taking along with him the good news of his first voyage. Six Indians were also taken along, as proof that he really had been to a land unknown to Europeans.

Columbus' achievement was not that he discovered new lands. In fact he did not. Columbus' rightful place in history is that he revealed to the rest of Europe the existence of lands and peoples across the Atlantic.

Columbus lived to make three other voyages. By his death in 1506 he had explored the entire Caribbean and parts of Middle America.

Early Spanish Governors

Spain appointed governors for her Caribbean colonies. Christopher Columbus and his brother Bartholomew were the first to govern in the Indies. They were soon to be relieved of the position and were succeeded by Francisco Bobadilla.

Bobadilla was succeeded by Nicholas Ovando in 1503. It was during his period of service that development began. Plants such as grapevine, olive, figs, lemons, wheat, rice, bananas, sugarcane and animals such as horses, cows, sheep, pigs and chickens were brought to the New World for the first time. The colony experienced remarkable growth under Ovando.

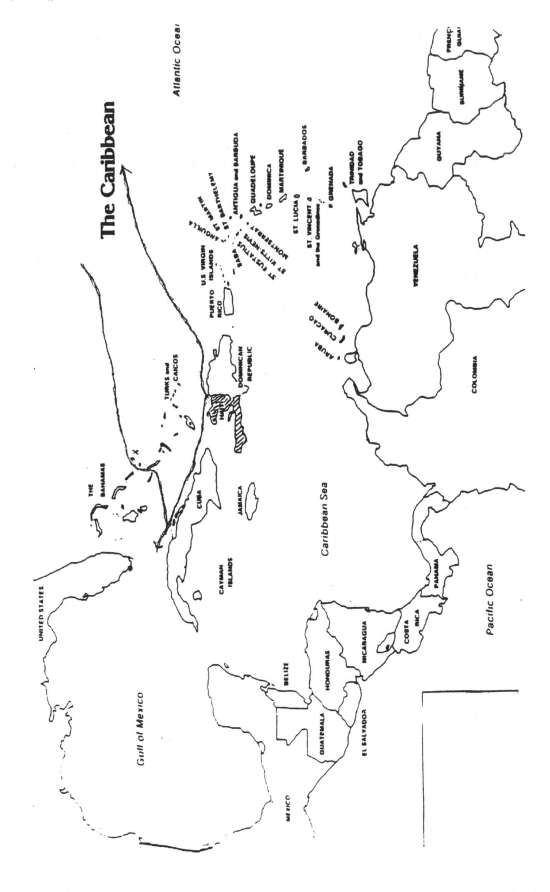

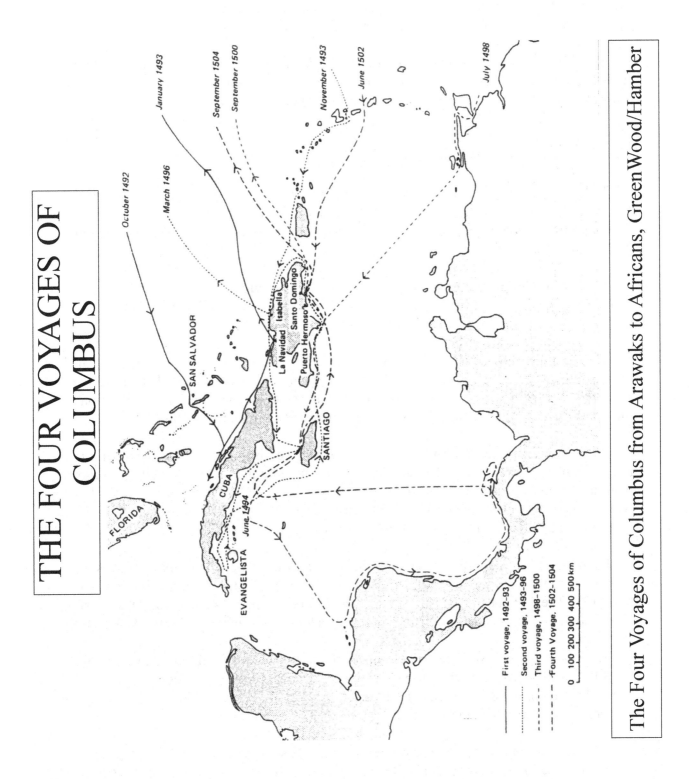

THE FOUR VOYAGES OF COLUMBUS

October 1492
March 1496
January 1493
September 1504
September 1500
November 1493
June 1502
July 1498

SAN SALVADOR
FLORIDA
CUBA
EVANGELISTA
June 1494
SANTIAGO
La Navidad Isabella
Santo Domingo
Puerto Hermoso

First voyage, 1492–93
Second voyage, 1493–96
Third voyage, 1498–1500
Fourth Voyage, 1502–1504
0 100 200 300 400 500km

The Four Voyages of Columbus from Arawaks to Africans, GreenWood/Hamber

Ovando was succeeded by Diego Columbus. It was during his period as governor that Cuba, Puerto Rico and Jamaica were settled. In 1509 de Esquivel invaded and conquered Jamaica; in 1511 Velasquez led an expedition to conquer Cuba, and in 1512 Ponce de Leon invaded and attempted the conquest of Puerto Rico.

By 1520, Spain was in control of the four islands of the Greater Antilles. Colonial development in the Caribbean led to a rapid decline and finally the destruction of the Arawaks—the original inhabitants of the (Caribbean) Greater Antilles.

The Spanish Speaking Caribbean

Today, the Spanish speaking Caribbean is comprised of Cuba, Puerto Rico, and the Dominican Republic—(the eastern two-thirds of Hispaniola). These were three of the first four places to be settled by Spain; Jamaica, the fourth Spanish Caribbean colony was captured by the British in 1655.

Spanish colonization in the New World began on Hispaniola in 1493. From that island, conquerors were sent to Puerto Rico (1508), Jamaica (1509) and Cuba (1511). All four colonies began as producers of agricultural commodities.

The conquest of the great Aztec Empire (1521) and the Inca Empire (1540), had far-reaching effects on the Caribbean. The discovery of gold and silver in Mexico and Peru resulted in a shift in Spain's interest, from the Caribbean to the mainland. The population of the Caribbean, and the islands' economic life experienced a dramatic decline.

By the middle of the sixteenth century, the islands had begun to experience a period of neglect. Cuba, Puerto Rica, and Hispaniola were now more important for strategic reasons than they were as producers of wealth. Jamaica was captured by the British in 1655; Haiti which was settled by the French in 1654 became a French possession officially in 1697, when it was ceded to France by the Treaty of Ryswick.

For the next 100 years Spain continued to control its Latin American Empire. As a result of revolutionary wars during the first quarters of the nineteenth century, Spain lost its mainland territories. The Caribbean islands were all that remained. Spain's control of Cuba became more and more repressive as the years passed. This led to the Ten Years' War. (1868-1878).

The relationship between Spain and Cuba continued to be hostile after the Ten Years' War. In 1895, patriotic Cubans such as Estrada Palma, Maceo and Jose Marti began a struggle for Cuban liberation. In 1898 the United States declared war on Spain and joined the liberation movement. The Spanish/American War lasted only a few months.

As a result of the war, Spain lost her Caribbean possessions. Cuba gained its independence in 1902 and Puerto Rico came under United States' control. A very strong economic relationship developed between Cuba and the United States. Puerto Rico moved from military control in

1900 to civilian government. In 1917, as a result of the Jones' Act, Puerto Ricans became citizens of the United States.

Over the past century, each of the former Spanish Caribbean colonies has followed its own path to development. However, their cultures all reflect very strong Iberian foundations, tempered by West African survivals.

They Were Here To Welcome Columbus

The Arawaks came from South America 3,000 years ago,
Where they were going they did not know.
Up from the mainland and on to Martinique,
They kept on moving, their freedom to seek.
Life of these Indians was of pleasure—not pain,
Their greatest concerns were Caribs and occasional hurricane.
 On their arrival the Spaniards met
A beautiful people, people you would never forget.

Some were fishermen, some worked the farm,
None that they met would they do harm.
The Spaniards reported that they were kind,
Gifts they made of all that they could find.
Shells and carvings and pieces of gold,
They gave all to the strangers—so we are told.
Generous they were with their time too,
They helped the Spaniards with whatever they had to do.

Religion these Indians also had,
They worshipped various types of earthly gods.
The Zemis were worshipped every day,
They were made of cotton, wood and pieces of clay.
The Cacique was judge, lawmaker and chief priest,
He served his people, from the nobility to the least.
His position passed down from father to son,
It was not earned by great deeds that he had done.

They were fishermen, farmers and hunters too.
Their favorite meal was a pepper-pot stew.
Fish and conchs, snakes and iguana,
Were favorite foods on Puerto Rico, Cuba and Jamaica.
The land was cleared by Arawak men,
The planting was left to the islands' women.
Children also had work to do,
The old and infirm made their contribution too.

Education was the business of the old,
Children learned through stories that they were told.
When work was over they had their fling,
Swimming and diving; they would dance and sing.
A good feast was enjoyed by the people all,
Their game, batos, was like volley ball.
Their simple laws they did obey,
In their beautiful villages on the bay.

When life on earth finally was done,
They went to a land beyond the sun.
 Dead Caciques were placed in caves.
They did not use our modern graves.
With food and tools and a favorite wife,
They were sent to Coyaba to begin a new life.
Coyaba was a place where there were no cares.
They didn't have to fear the Caribs' spears.

Thus it was when the Spaniards came,
Never would it be the same again.
Enslavement and diseases the strangers brought,
All they cared for was the gold they sought.
Soon all the Arawaks from the islands were gone.
Leaving behind them none to mourn.
And so it was the way was paved,
For West African arrivals, their souls to save.

Spanish Colonization
They Came To Save Souls

To the West! To the West! To the West we must go!
The good Lord Almighty hath appointed it so!
Thousands and thousands of souls to be won,
Savages to be saved as soon as we can.
Children of God they too might be,
All that they lack is Christianity.

Thus for another voyage preparations began,
Farmer and seed, soldier and gun.
Seventeen ships and fifteen hundred men,
Ready to sail to the Caribbean again.
Safe and sound the ships did arrive,
With all aboard very much alive.

Columbus returned as a triumphant leader,
A settlement he established—he called Isabella.
For the religion they were promised the Indians had to pay,
Hard work in the mines was exacted every day.
Thus the number of Indians steadily declined,
As a result of work in those wretched gold mines.

The Spaniards' dreams were never fulfilled,
Though innocent Indians were unnecessarily killed.
The settlers requested an able governor,
And so they sent Francisco Bobadilla.
Christopher Columbus lost his pride of place,
And returned to Spain in utter disgrace.

Columbus' return to Spain in chains
Caused the Queen to wonder if Bobadilla was insane.
The Queen decided that Bobadilla had to go,
So she appointed Governor Nicholas de Ovando.
Ovando proved to be a very smart man,
He saw a bright future in the fertile land.

Soon the colony from destruction was saved,
The way to the future Ovando had paved.
Agricultural success had its dismal side,
Haiti's Indians perished like thousands of flies.
Thus the success of Spanish agriculture
Rested on a system of slavery called Encomienda.

Bartholomew De Las Casas soon realized
That Spanish policies needed to be revised.
To the Church and Crown this Priest did appeal,
He was shocked with what his queries would reveal.
Church, Crown and Spanish settler
Supported the brutal Encomienda!

To save the Indians Las Casas did suggest,
That slaves could be obtained from Africa's West.
The Crown and Church were soon to agree,
That West African people would cross the sea.
African enslavement thus had begun
And Arawak culture was soon to be gone.

So it was that the slave trade did begin,
Africans too were to be saved from their sins.
Trip after trip the slave ships did make,
Kings and peasants the slave traders did take.
The Spanish demand the Portuguese did supply,
So long as Spain had the money to buy.

As time went by colonial rulers were changed,
Of interest and talents there was a wide range.
In 1509 Diego did arrive
Caribbean policies were his to decide.
Islands of the seas he wished to explore,
Before he was recalled he would settle some more.

In 1509 to Puerto Rico De Leon did go,
Spanish might to the Indians he wanted to show.
That same year an expedition De Esquivel did lead—
To Jamaica to sow yet another Spanish seed.
Cuba was the last of the Greater Antilles,
To join the ranks of the West Indian colonies.

Agricultural prosperity continued to grow.
Soon from the colonies there was much to show
Sugar and citrus, tallow and hides,
There was little gold from the Spanish mines.

71

The early explorers had played their part.
They had given to Spain a very good start.
The British, the French and the Dutch people too,
Disliked what was happening but knew not what to do.
They had to abide by the Pope's dictates.
If they failed, the Pope could excommunicate.
So dear reader, the stage was finally set
What would happen next, I guess you could bet.

At this stage it is important to understand
How the first Africans became West Indians.
West Africans arrived a hundred years or more.
Before Africans were brought to North America's shores
If slavery in America you wish to understand,
Go back to the Caribbean, that's where it began.

Overnight Success

The spirit of adventure continued apace
Spain was running a one horse race.
In 1509 Balboa visited Panama,
On the other side of the Isthmus—the Pacific he saw.
He established a city he called Darien
He wondered at Indian mysteries again and again.

Balboa opened wide the mainland's door,
Soon would follow other Conquistadores.
In 1512 De Leon sailed north,
He hoped to find the Fountain of Youth.
He passed Bimini and at Florida did stop,
The Florida Peninsula was now on the map.

Velasquez of Cuba important Governor was he,
Hernando Cortez was his secretary.
The conquistador's life Cortez did prefer
A trading to Mexico Cortez would go.
To Mexico, Cortez, Velasquez did send,
On his secretary, Velasquez thought he could depend.

Cortez had secretly planned to over-throw
The Aztec empire and open North America's door.
The fall of Mexico is an interesting story,
It's one of the strangest in North American history.
In the interest of space, suffice it to say,
It opened to Spain a brand new day.

Gold and silver they found galore,
Ship load after shipload and still there was more.
Another culture was soon to be destroyed,
What was once a great city was now simply void.
The Aztec people were also enslaved,
The way to Spanish colonization, here again was paved.

Next, the Spaniards moved to Peru.
The Inca Empire they destroyed too.
Gold and silver in quantities abound
Rich were the lands the Spaniards had found.
Of Incas, like Aztecs slaves the Spaniards did make
While their gold and silver they daily did take.

Spain overnight had certainly become
In wealth and in power, Europe's number one.
Other nations of Europe stood idly by—
The reason for this you already know why.
The Pope was still Europe's most powerful man.
He held the power of ex-communication.

Heros Of Latin America

From the very beginning of the development of what would later become the United States of America people of Latin America had been making their contributions to this nation.

The last 50 years have seen a dramatic increase in the migration of Latin American and Caribbean peoples to the United States of America. The growth in the number of people from Latin America is having and will continue to have far reaching effects on the future of the nation socially, economically, and politically.

It is therefore high time that more serious attention be paid to the history and culture of Latin American and Caribbean peoples.

It is only by so doing that the youth of the nation will come to understand and appreciate the contributions of Latin Americans to the history of the Americas in general (over the last 500 years), and to the history of the United States in particular.

The poem—Heroes of Latin American—introduces some outstanding Latin American leaders. A study of the life of each will reveal that where there is commitment, courage and concern for the betterment of the conditions of the lives of a people change will result.

Heros Of Latin America

From Latin America these heroes did come,
To make their mark on History through victories they won.
Marcus Garvey was a great Pan-Africanist,
Pedro Albizu Campos Puerto Rican nationalist.

Toussaint L'Overture Haiti's great general
Jose Marti, Cuba's hero/poet with liberation plan.
Simon Bolivar military genius was he,
Liberator of Latin America he fought to be.

Estrada Palma, Cuba's independence was the goal he sought.
Antonio Maceo, Cuba for Cubans, the time had come at last.
Goodbye Spain, goodbye America
Welcome home you fair people of Cuba.

For Chile, Peru, Argentina he fought,
His people's freedom was the goal he sought.
The land he loved he tried to win,
Argentina's son, Jose San Marti.

Father Hidalgo—Oh what a Man!
He rallied the Indians to reclaim the land.
In spite of the fact that his mission did fail,
His name forever Mexicans will hail.

These are but few of the leaders of the past,
About whom fond memories forever will last.
Today to South Florida people of their lands do come,
Open your hearts and bid them welcome.

CHAPTER-5

CHALLENGE TO SPAIN'S POWER

The British In The Caribbean

Growth Of The English Speaking Caribbean

It was from Guiana that the first settlers came to start the first British colony in the Caribbean—St. Kitts (1624). St. Kitts (St. Christopher) would soon be followed by Antigua, Montserrat, Nevis and Barbados (1625-1630). All these new British colonies began as tobacco producers, but soon became sugar producers.

The Dutch had little interest in establishing colonies. However, they had a great interest in colonization. The Dutch were more interested in shipping and commerce. They therefore lent the British and French money to develop colonies, taught them how to grow and manufacture sugar and provided transportation to take the sugar back to Europe. The Dutch hoped that by providing such services to the British and the French they would gain great benefits later.

In 1655, during the reign of Oliver Cromwell, the British attempted to take Spain's most important colony—Hispaniola. Failing to take Hispaniola, the British attacked and captured Jamaica.

British control of islands such as St. Lucia, Tobago, St. Vincent, Dominica and Grenada came later. These islands were either settled or claimed by the French, but became British as a result of treaties such as The Treaties of Paris (1763), Versailles (1783) and Vienna (1815), which ended European conflicts.

Trinidad, which had been under Spanish control since the early 16th Century, became a place of refuge for French and Irish settlers during the Napoleonic Wars. When finally the war ended, Trinidad became a part of the British Empire. (Treaty of Vienna, 1815).

The limits of the English speaking Caribbean were drawn by 1815. By 1815 Britain controlled St. Kitts, Nevis, Antigua, Bahamas, Jamaica, St. Lucia, Tobago, St. Vincent, Dominica, Grenada, Guiana (South America) and Trinidad.

It is important to note that most of these islands were formerly owned either by France or Spain. It should not be surprising, therefore, to find differing degrees of Spanish or French influence throughout the English-speaking Caribbean.

Bahamas

The Bahamas became British in 1648. In that year a group of settlers from Bermuda (British) settled on the island of Eleuthera. The development of the Bahamas was slow. The most remarkable thing about the Bahamas in the early years was its reputation as a home for sea rovers. Governor Woodes Rogers did much to suppress piracy and establish legitimate trade. In 1629 he introduced Assembly Government.

It was not until 1783 that the Bahamas embarked on a new path to development. Between 1783 and 1789 about 8,000 Loyalists and their enslaved Africans sought refuge in the Bahamas. This was the result of the successful war waged by the former 13 North American colonies against England for their independence; the result was the birth of a new nation—the U.S.A.

The population of the Bahamas increased in six years (1783-1789) by 200%, from 4,000 to 12,000 (Deans Peggs). As a result of the introduction of new capital along with people with new ideas, the social, economic and political life of the Bahamas experienced significant changes. The white minority became the ruling elite controlling the islands well into the 20th Century.

In spite of numerous problems faced by the black majority, problems such as lack of educational and economic opportunities, the majority of the population survived by turning to the land and sea. By the middle of the 20th century, the Bahamas was experiencing significant social, political and economic changes.

Freeport the nation's second city was established. It acted like a magnet, attracting people from the less developed islands and from abroad. It attracted investment capital and soon became a major industrial center in the northern Bahamas. Freeport became a major tourist destination also. By the 1960's the Bahamas was experiencing full employment.

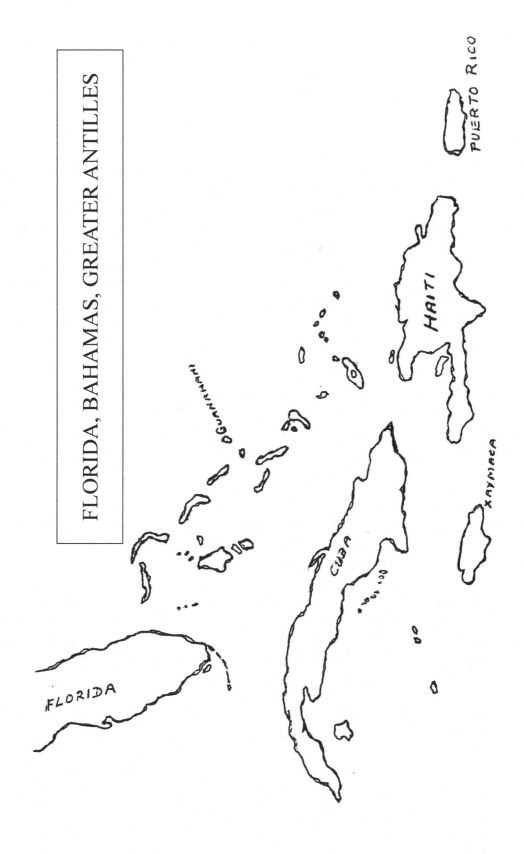

FLORIDA, BAHAMAS, GREATER ANTILLES

Piracy In The Bahamas

Some were fat and some were thin,
Always in a battle they fought to win.
Some were short and some were tall,
Always ready at their captain's call.
Some tied their heads, some wore hats,
Some owned parrots and some owned cats.

Some were young and some were old,
As a group they all were bold.
Some were captains and some were crew,
What they liked most were the waters blue.
Some were women and some were men,
Sword they had instead of pen.

Pistols and shots carried by the score,
Cutlass and axes they had—to be sure.
Some wore shoes and some wore boots,
All of them were lovers of Spanish loot.
At sea as well as on land
They were feared by all nations.

As privateers and buccaneers some had begun,
Soon they realized piracy was more fun.
French men, English men and Dutch men too
All sailed the waters of the Caribbean blue.
Spain paid the price of pirates action,
Whether at sea or whether on land.

Mary Reid and Ann Bonney by name,
Were female pirates of very great fame.
Dressed as men they took their place,
Seeing in piracy no disgrace.
Then in battle,—who won't remember?
They claimed no privilege because of gender.

Lloyd E. Afflick

Reckless and ruthless they called these men,
Jennings and Vane and the rest of them.
Generous and kind they sometimes could be,
Disciplined as soldiers while at sea.
Live for the moment was their lives' great plan,
No thought of the future or of the life beyond.

Hell on earth of Nassau they made,
Soon they stopped legitimate trade.
Spanish anger they brought to a boil.
Proprietary plans they certainly did foil.
Severe pressure on Britain was brought to bear,
From the Bahamas these pirates to urgently clear.

A man of great fame as governor was he,
As rough and tough as pirates could be.
A son and grandson of men of the sea,
His job he performed quite efficiently.
Woodes Rogers—the name of this great man,
He brought much change to this our land.

In 1718 Woodes Rogers from England did come,
Law and Order was his aim number one.
Conditions in the Bahamas in 1720,
Closely resembled full blown anarchy.

Fishers and farmers many pirates did become,
Life on the sea was no longer fun.
A chapter of excitement I'm sure you'll agree,
In this story of ours—Bahamian History.

The Bahamian Society

Period of Settlement

The arrival of the Spaniards in the New World in 1492 had disastrous effects on the people of the Caribbean in general and the Bahamas in particular. By 1540 the 30, 000 Bahamian Lucayan Indians were all transported to Hispaniola where they died in mines and on plantations.

The islands remained uninhabited until 1648 when 70 new Puritan settlers arrived from Bermuda. The size of this new settlement and the conditions under which the settlers lived (ship-wrecked refugees) made only a low level of stratification possible (male, female roles).

The society grew slowly experiencing Proprietary control, Piracy and finally structured government under the control of a Royal Governor by 1729. It was at this stage that stratification developed. At the top of the society was a group responsible for the administration of the affairs of the colony and answerable to Britain. This group was comprised of the governor, his council men and their friends who formed the upper class. Below this group was a group of working men (fishers, woodcutters, wreckers) who were the majority of the then white society.

At the bottom was a group of slaves who could not hope for betterment of their condition. They existed in a caste like status. The population in 1731 was made up of 925 whites and 453 blacks giving a total of 1,738 persons. (A History of the Bahamas, Michael Craton, 1986, page 116) Bahamian population increased slowly until 1783 when the population was estimated to be 4,000.

The Coming Of The Loyalists

Persecution in the USA after the American War of Independence resulted in the coming of over 7,000 Loyalists and slaves to the 3ahamas. In less than six years the Bahamian population increased by nearly 200 percent from a total of 4,000 in 1784 to a total of 11,300 in 1789.

This dramatic population increase had far reaching effects on the Bahamian society. Britain granted the new comers over 42,000 acres of land which became the basis for a new cotton plantation system in the Bahamas. (Craton, 1986, page 151)

Many of the Loyalists were professional and business people. The imposition of an educated elite on a fishing village type community naturally led to conflict. The old established white society did not take kindly to the pressures applied by the new comers. The new comers in turn could not accept the leadership of a group of uneducated fishermen. Conflict resulting from class interests finally was resolved when the new comers assumed power.

By the beginning of the 19th century the Loyalists had established control over large tracts of land and had developed a cotton plantation type of economy. To protect their class interests the Loyalists gradually gained control of the machinery of government.

Cotton production led to further increase in the number of slaves. Fear of slave uprisings led to the passage of severe slave codes. The caste system became even more rigid.

The social structure by 1820 was made up of a powerful white elite (Loyalists from the USA) a powerless white sea fearing class. The Black population after1808 became quite complex. There were the descendants of the slaves who had been in the Bahamas since the time of settlement; there were others who were brought in from the Caribbean and Africa and sold in the slave market; and there were those who had been brought to the Bahamas by the Loyalists. The last group of Blacks to arrive was a group of free Blacks who were taken from slave ships by the British navy between 1811 and1860. By 1860 this group amounted to 6098 persons (Journal of the Bahamas Historical Society; vol. 4 number 1 October 1982.

In the eyes of the whites there was no difference between one Black and another

The Colonial Context

In analyzing the development of the Bahamian social structure, it is important to bear in mind that between 1648 and 1973 the archipelago was a colony of Britain. As a colony a dependent relationship existed between the Bahamas and the mother country. All important decisions had to have the approval of Britain.

Although from the economic point of view the Bahamas was not as important as the sugar colonies to the south, (ex.) Barbados and Jamaica, in an era of imperial rivalry^ Britain maintained it's control over the Bahamas at all cost. British governors ruled over the islands throughout most of their history to ensure that British interests were protected.

Internal developments over the centuries should therefore be seen as taking place within this colonial context where final power rested in the hands of external rulers.

The settlement of the Loyalists between 1783 and 1789 which changed the direction of Bahamian history was the result of a British decision. The development of Nassau as a trans-shipment port for guns, ammunition and other war supplies for the Confederate forces during the American Civil War was also an example of Britain effecting it's foreign policy decisions through the use of the Bahamas.

The exploitation of the Black masses by a white minority for over 200 years was done with the assent of Britain, since governors were appointed to see that colonies were properly governed.

As late as 1955 a major decision which will affect the Bahamas forever was made by the white minority government supported by the imperial power. That decision, The Hawkesbill Creek Agreement led to the establishment of Freeport.

In spite of the short term economic, benefits of Freeport, the leaders of the* opposing forces to the then Bahamian and British governments expressed without reservations their disgust with the agreement which had been arrived at.

As late as 1968 the leader of the former white minority government Sir Roland Symonette expressed his party's delight in the relationship between Britain and the Bahamas. Sir Roland stated "The Bahama Islands, one of the oldest and most loyal territories of her majesty are proud of their long connection with the United Kingdom, and we the United Bahamian Party strongly desire that this association should continue not only because we are loyal British subjects, but also for a more selfish reason-it is our opinion and firm belief that independence is not in the best interest of the people of the Bahama Islands." (Quiet Revolution, Doctor Doris Johnson 1972, page131)

In considering the development of the Bahamas therefore, it should be bourn in mind that until 1973 when the Bahamas achieved independence, real power resided in Britain. The minority white government was able to maintain control simply because its policies synchronized with the policies of the imperial power. British colonial control and local policies were the forces which played the most significant role in shaping the Bahamian social structure.

Modern Bahamas

As time passed the islands developed as a British colony with a way of life peculiar to its historical roots. By the 1950's the Bahamas had begun to produce new leadership from its Black majority.

Bahamian nationalism had become a major aspect of the colony's political development. The impact of the American Civil Rights Movement, awareness of political changes across the Caribbean, and the desire of the Bahamian majority to take their colony in a new direction led to increasing demands of a social and economic nature.

New emphasis was placed on economic and educational development. As mentioned earlier, by the 1960's the Bahamas was experiencing full employment. Thanks to the city of Freeport which had become a major industrial and tourist center. On July 10, 1973 the Bahamas became an independent nation. It continued its Parliamentary Democratic form of Government begun nearly two and a half centuries earlier.

Today the Bahamas is one of the World's leading tourist destinations. It's beautiful beaches, ideal climatic conditions, world-class hotels and friendly, hospitable people are among its major attractions.

The Tobacco Economy (In The Caribbean)

Britain's first colony was little St. Kitts,
It was producing tobacco by 1624
Soon it was joined by Nevis, Antigua, and Montserrat,
They all produced tobacco; please remember that.

The early settlers of the Caribbean carefully chose,
A crop for export on which they could not lose.
There were cocoa and coffee, cotton and dyes,
These were forsaken; tobacco won the prize.

Tobacco became crop number one,
 Of all the crops of the Caribbean.
Raleigh had seen the Indians smoke—
So he introduced it to the British folk.

The colony of Virginia had set the pace,
In tobacco production Virginia had the 'ace'.
When tobacco production the Caribbean did begin,
 A great competition naturally set in.

Tobacco production the planters did emphasize,
They had to consider, population size.
Slowness, spoilage and irregularity
Were points to be considered about crossing the sea.

The wealthy of Europe wanted luxury goods,
To supply these, the settlers did the best that they could.
Tobacco smoking was becoming fashionable,
It could easily be supplied; it was not perishable.

Great profits from tobacco the settlers did make
Naturally, the other crops they did forsake.
Tobacco was ideal at the beginning of the century,
It was a time of limited technology.

A man and family could export,
To pay for their limited European import.
Then if their abilities, their needs did exceed
Indentured workers were recruited, as many as there was need.

Virginia's production certainly did exceed Caribbean tobacco.
Virginia had the lead; combined production had created a glut,
The Caribbean supply had to be cut.

An economic crisis the colonies did face,
How would they survive in this little place?
Possible exports, there was quite a few
Which to select they wished they knew.

Then from Brazil the answer came,
The replacement crop was the sugar cane.
To the Dutch, the British owed their gratitude,
They were saved from disaster in these latitudes.

A Funny Story—The Capture Of Jamaica

From time to time in History,
You will come across a funny story.
This certainly was Jamaica's case;
Let's hear the story, there is no time to waste.
This really is an interesting comedy,
Read on dear reader and you will see.

In 1649 King Charles lost his head,
Cromwell was happy, the King was dead.
Cromwell took charge of political affairs,
And ruled Britain for nine long years.
Oliver Cromwell really hated Spain,
And planned to destroy her, by the end of his reign.

He put together an elaborate plan,
 "Against Spain I'll do the best that I can".
The plan was called his "Western Design"
Britain's prestige was put on the line.
Protestant Britain against Catholic Spain,
Cromwell had eyes on the Spanish Main.

First, his enemy he planned to confront,
Of a British victory he had no doubt.
The Spanish monarch he promised to punish,
If he refused to grant Cromwell his wish.
"To British traders you will open your ports,
British inter-lopers release from your forts."

"To the island of Tortuga the buccaneers have rights,
Leave them alone or there will be a fight"
When in response, Spain showed no positive sign,
Cromwell put into effect his "Western Design".
Cromwell had eyes on the Spanish Main,
He planned to destroy that Catholic Spain.

Cromwell badly under-rated Spanish power,
He thought Spain had just a "sham" Empire.

Real soldiers he sent were a thousand or less,
From the streets of London he gathered the rest.
His Commanders were Venables and Admiral Perm,
Britain's best soldiers he refused to send.

Thirty-eight ships under a disciplined crew,
Gracefully sailed, into the ocean blue.
This most important British expedition
Sailed directly to the Caribbean.
Definite orders? There really were none.
"When the mission is over make sure you've won".

The expedition did finally arrive,
In February sixteen fifty five.
Farmers, tradesmen and an occasional buccaneer
Were soon a part of 3,000 volunteers.
St. Kitts, Nevis and Montserrat,
All did contribute to that motley lot.

Barbados too, contributed its share,
Let it not be said, "Barbados didn't care"
Finally they sailed in April 1655,
In a Spanish port, they were soon to arrive.
A conquering force, nine thousand strong,
Hoped to capture some Spanish land.

Men, There were more than enough,
But what about other military stuff?
Some basic discipline they certainly could use,
Appropriate clothing and proper shoes.
"How can I fight without sword or gun?
The up-coming battle certainly will be no fun."

And so for Hispaniola the fleet did sail,
Poorly disciplined and ill-prepared.
The British plan was a terrible mistake,
When Hispaniola they decided to take.
Hispaniola was a Spanish strong-hold,
Cromwell seemed not to have been told.

On April 14, the British went ashore,
Nine thousand strong, possibly more.
To Santo Domingo they did advance,
Little did they know they had no chance.

Of their coming the Spaniards were all aware,
For the up-coming battle they were well prepared.

Santo Domingo they finally reached,
After a few days journey from the tropical beach.
A single charge from Spanish cavalry men,
Sent the British running back to the beach again.
They had come this far to stand and fight,
Now Spaniards had them in hopeless flight.

Finally they were back at the landing place,
Trembling in terror, it was a national disgrace!
To England the leaders dare not return,
When of their failure Cromwell did learn.
They could not report on the mission they had led,
They feared that Cromwell might chop off their heads.

They failed to win a very great prize,
A place of importance in the Spaniards eyes.
To Jamaica the survivors nervously sailed,
Hoping that this time they would not fail.
The Spaniards, on seeing the British fleet,
Did not think twice—they took to their feet.

The Spanish colonists to the hills did run,
They did not swing a sword or fire a gun.
A few remained to receive the terms of surrender,
Beautiful Jamaica! There was not one to defend her.
And so it was that the British did gain,
It's largest colony in the Caribbean chain.

Penn and Venables felt much relieved,
Their disgraceful former failure they tried to conceal.
They returned to England, proud of their conquest
What happened next you would never guess.
Oliver Cromwell threw them in jail,
And that is the end of our comical tale.

The leaders of the expedition disobeyed their command,
They should have remained and settle the island.
Jamaica they left under Colonel D' Oyley,
Who for 15 years was busy as a bee.
He was constantly defending Britain's new colony
From Spaniards who returned from across the sea.

The Spanish Crown finally agreed,
To the clauses and terms of the Treaty of Madrid.
After years of trying, Spain eventually realized,
That the time had come to sever its ties.
And so it happened in sixteen seventy,
Jamaica became Britain's officially.

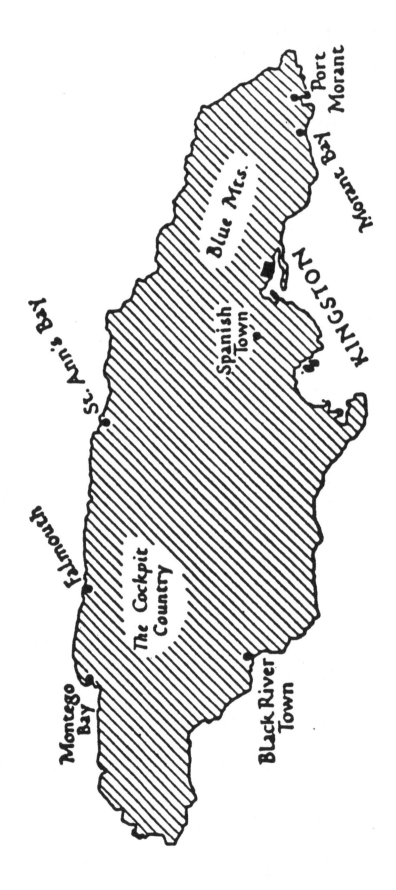

Jamaica To The Rescue

In the Eastern Caribbean, all worthwhile land
Had found its way into the planters' hand.
Everything possible annually was done,
To squeeze from every acre, every possible ton.
Yet as much as the planters tried,
Their customers quite often could not be supplied.
What action could Caribbean planters take,
In their factories more sugar to make?

In Europe, demand for sugar continued to increase,
In the Caribbean, supply of land continued to decrease.
Thus it was in sixteen fifty-five
Jamaica became colony of the largest size.
 From Barbados, St. Kitts, Nevis and Montserrat,
Came new settlers to new sugar plots.
For the rest of the century Jamaica's growth was slow,
The reason for this you now should know.

Jamaica developed an unusual fame,
Its leading citizens it could not tame.
It became headquarters of British buccaneers,
They came from Providence, Tortuga and even here.
The settlers in the Caribbean could not live in peace,
Unless in Jamaica buccaneering ceased.
By the turn of the century the buccaneers were gone,
Thanks to a former leader, Henry Morgan.

Peace in Jamaica was restored at last,
 Providing an opportunity to the planter class.
Numerous plantations were established on the plains,
From sugar, remember, there was much to be gained.
Of the sugar producing islands, Jamaica became number one,
Thanks to the abundance and fertility of her land.
West African people provided the labor force,
Investment capital came from Britain of course.

And so in the Caribbean new societies were born,
The original people? Remember they were all gone.
New customs from Africa these people did bring,
Their music, their dance, their ability to sing.
And so dear reader, I hope you'll understand,
The impact of sugar in the Caribbean.
What began in such an accidental way,
Has remained a pillar of the economy till this very day.

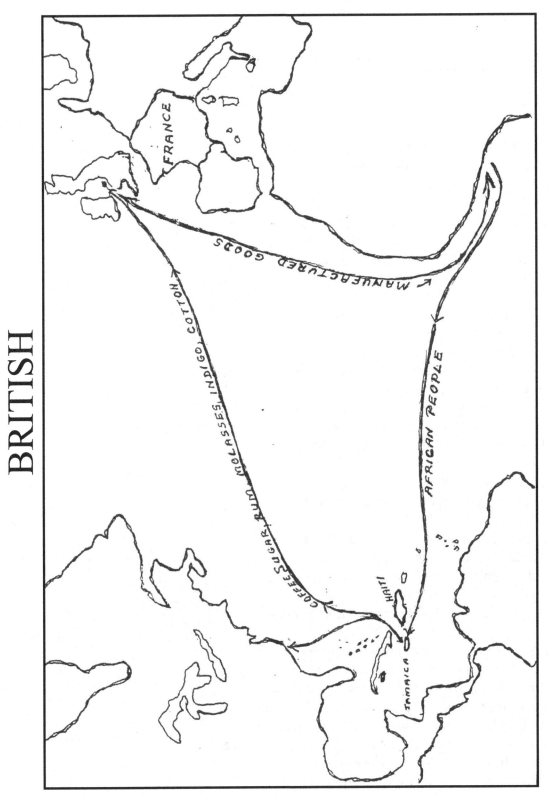

BRITISH

THE TRIANGULAR TRADE

The Mercantile System

By 1652 the world had changed,
In every way to Britain's advantage.
England and France, Portugal and Spain,
Had crossed the seas for colonial gain.
In North America, Africa and India too,
Were places over which the Union Jack flew.
St. Kitts, Nevis, Barbados and Montserrat,
Were islands of the West Indies, Britain had got.

The island of Jamaica was soon to become,
The major producer of sugar and rum.
In matters of trade the Dutch were first,
They were the world's leader in international commerce.
Britain disliked the growing trend,
The Dutch's commerce she wished to end.
In 1652 Navigation Laws were passed,
The aim was to expel the Dutch at last.

All her colonies Britain did arrange,
In a system devised for matters of trade.
Goods from the colonies were officially banned,
From transportation in ships from foreign lands.
Africans were brought across the sea,
India supplied America with eastern tea.
The West Indies produced sugar and rum,
Britain supplied all with ammunition and gun.

All were locked in a commercial system,
The system was called—Mercantilism.
Prices for her products the British controlled,
Prices for their products the colonists were told.
Against Britain no colony dared to compete,
Their daily demands the Mother Country would meet.
Year after year the system went on,
This system of colonial exploitation.

The fortunes made from colonial plantations,
Were used to finance Britain's Industrial Revolution.
A ship building industry the system did stimulate,
A navy was trained for the defense of the State.
Britain had surpassed France and Spain,
In wealth, power, prestige and international fame.
To colonial sufferings Britain turned a blind eye,
In Africa and the Caribbean people suffered and died.

Finally from the colonies enough money was made,
Mercantilism was abandoned, it was time for Free Trade.
Against Britain, there was none to compete,
She had many industries and a great shipping fleet.
"Open your doors and let us in,
It is time for international competition to begin."
And so it was that the foundation was laid,
For a new economic system called Free Trade.

Britain's interest in industrialization,
Explains the decline of the sugar plantations.
For over a century humanitarians had tried,
Yet freedom for slaves Britain had denied.
It is difficult to explain Britain's change of heart,
Unless you understand the economic part.
The sugar colonies were important no more,
Her future now depended on coal and iron ore.

So dear reader, I hope you have seen,
The shifting fortunes of the Caribbean.
In 1838 a new period began,
The slaves were freed without any land.
How would slaves use this new found liberty?
First they had to establish an identity.
Their traditional culture for centuries they were denied.
Yet, much which was African managed to survive.

Gone were their languages, titles and names,
Still surviving were their stories, music and games.
Riddles and proverbs and a "sense of community"
Helped to shape their New World identity.
Together they worked and together they played,
Building communities without any aid.
And so over time, descendants of Africans,
Gradually became modern West Indians.

CHAPTER-6

LATER CARIBBEAN DEVELOPMENT

Jamacia
The Sugar Revolution And After

Jamaica was occupied by the Spaniards between 1509 and 1655. During those years, the island developed as a ranching colony. <u>In 1655 the island was captured by the British.</u> Shortly after the capture; the Spaniards fled to Cuba leaving their slaves behind, it was these slaves who were responsible for the establishment of free communities in the mountains of Jamaica and were later called Maroons.

The capture of Jamaica was a blessing in disguise for the former tobacco planters of the Eastern Caribbean, who had lost their land when sugar replaced tobacco as the export crop during the 1640s and 1650s. Hundreds of settlers from islands such as St Kitts, Nevis, Montserrat, Antigua, Barbados arrived in Jamaica to begin life anew.

Sugar cultivation got off to a slow start in Jamaica as buccaneering became the chief

feature of Jamaican life during the first 20 years after the island's capture. Buccaneering came to a dramatic end when, in 1692, an earthquake destroyed Port Royal.

By the beginning of the eighteenth century the sugar plantation-system was well established and was setting the stage for Jamaica's future development. The first 75 years of the eighteenth century were years of growth. As the number of acres under sugar increased, so did the number of Africans who were brought in to be enslaved and to work on the plantations. Jamaica had become the leading producer of sugar in the British West Indies by 1775.

Slaves were not permitted to take their material things from Africa with them. Great attempts were made to destroy their culture. In spite of such efforts much of the African culture did survive. For example, music, dance, many every day expressions, beliefs, riddles and the love for stories, especially Anancy Stories.

The most profitable days of the sugar plantation system came to an end during the 1770s. In 1775 the North American colonies declared their independence and rebelled against Britain. This led to a disruption of the trade between North America and the Caribbean. This disruption of trade and the imposition of the Navigation Acts against the new USA led to shortages of plantation supplies and greatly inflated prices. Many planters were driven out of business. Only the most efficient planters survived.

Among the plantation supplies which had experienced severe increase in price were— salt beef, salt pork, corn and other commodities used to feed the slaves. In an attempt to reduce cost, the breadfruit, ackee and mangoes were brought to Jamaica to be used to feed the slaves. Today these items are very important in the diets of most Jamaicans.

Throughout the history of slavery, children were born to parents of British and African backgrounds. From among the children and grand children of this group came some of Jamaica's earliest lawyers, journalists, doctors and later political leaders.

In 1807 Britain passed a law ending the slave trade and in 1838 as a result of changing economic circumstances and the pressure of humanitarians, slavery ended.

HUMANITARIANS/ ABOLITIONISTS

Thomas Clarkson

Granville Sharpe

William Wilberforce

Sir Thomas Fowell Buxton

The New Society

With the exception of the Negro Education Grant (1835) of £30,000 for the colonies, and the Lady Mico Charity which was used to fund the Mico College for the training of teachers, no provision was made for the social welfare of the newly freed slaves. However, through cooperative efforts, and with the help of Missionaries, many former slaves were able to obtain land and start anew as independent peasant farmers. Others squatted on crown lands where they produced food for themselves and for sale in the market.

Ever since the 1770s the planters were experiencing severe problems resulting from rising cost of production and competition for market by other sugar producers such as Haiti. The planters problems were compounded when emancipation came. How would the plantation system survive without slave labor? A new supply of labor had to be found.

After attempting to obtain labor from among the newly freed Blacks from Europe, Africa, North America and Madeira, the planters turned their attention to China. Many Chinese came to Jamaica as indentured servants. The Chinese scheme failed however, because it was too expensive and the Chinese preferred commercial ventures to plantation labor and left as soon as they could.

Jamaica's sugar plantation system was saved by the immigration of Indians. Between the 1840s and 1917 when the scheme ended, an estimated total of 33,000 Indians were brought to Jamaica. Indian labor proved to be both reliable and cheap. Today many Indians whose great grandfathers came as indentured servants are playing very important roles in the Jamaican society.

The Morant Bay Rebellion And After

In 1865 an event took place in Jamaica which changed the course of the island's history. A series of poor harvests resulting from droughts, high prices, food shortage and governmental neglect caused a social uprising which has gone down in Jamaica's history as the Morant Bay Rebellion.

As a result of the Morant Bay Rebellion, George William Gordon, peacemaker and humanitarian who tried to prevent the rebellion and its bloody aftermath was hanged by the British for his efforts. Paul Bogle, the ex-slave who led the land hungry peasants in a demonstration against the social and economic conditions was deemed to have instigated the rebellion and "Deacon" Bogle, like Gordon was branded a traitor by the British and also hanged. Both men gave their lives in an attempt to better the condition of the Jamaican people. Today they are both honored as National Heroes.

The Morant Bay rebellion also had far reaching effects on the Jamaican political System. Fearing that they would not be able to continue to run the government of Jamaica after the rebellion, the Assembly voted itself out of existence, leaving it to the British to decide what form of government the island should have. In 1866 Crown Colony government was introduced under the guidance of the very capable governor—Sir John Peter Grant

Sir John Peter Grant effected many social, economic, and political reforms. However, when he left office a period of political decline set in. Jamaica's political life from the mid 1880s until 1944 was dominated by the struggle between Jamaicans on the one hand and Britain on the other over the question of Crown Colony Government

The worldwide economic crisis which resulted from the Great Depression (1929-1932) brought Jamaica's social, economic and political troubles to a head. What began as protests and demonstrations in 1938 developed into confrontation and violence. It was out of this situation that Jamaica got two of its earliest political leaders, Alexander Bustamante, and Norman Manley. Both men would later become National Heroes.

Rt. Excellent Norman Washington Manley

Sir Alexander Bustamante

In 1944 Jamaica was granted Universal Adult Suffrage, that is, the right of all persons over twenty one years old to vote. After 1944 the island moved gradually towards independence. For many years Caribbean leaders had given thought to the formation of a West Indian Federation. In 1958 the English speaking Caribbean finally came together under the banner of a Federal Government. From the very beginning this form of government was beset with problems. By 1962 the question for Jamaica was whether or not to federate. The matter soon became a local political party issue. It was put to the people in the form of a referendum. The voters showed their preference to "go it alone". On August 6, 1962, Jamaica became an independent nation. It was the first of the English speaking Caribbean islands to obtain the right of self determination.

Today Jamaica is a land with a rich and complex culture. Its people are the descendants of the various groups which came at different times under different circumstances. Each group has made its contribution to the Jamaican way of life. Many of the island's institutions, example, the political system, judicial system, education system, etc, are of British origin. Although English is the official language, historical circumstances have given rise to a dialect which is used by most people in their day to day communications. It is also commonly used in storytelling, music, (reggae) and poetry writing. (Louise Bennet, Mutabaruka).

In an attempt to provide employment for as many of its people as possible, Jamaica has been making great efforts to diversify its economy. However, bauxite mining, light industries, tourism and agriculture continue to be the major industries. Jamaica's major agricultural exports are sugar, coffee and banana. Cattle, pigs, goats and chickens are reared for local consumption.

Like most Caribbean countries, Jamaica has its share of social and economic problems. However, the island's people face the future with confidence.

The Sugar Revolution

By 1640 a new age had begun,
The 'crop competition' sugar had won.
 Never again would the islands be the same,
The islands would grow in wealth and fame.
Honey was the sweetener for many a century,
Sugar was now needed for coffee and tea.
British planters were willing, the demand to supply,
Since sugar price in Europe was very high.

They had no knowledge, but they had the will,
So they turned to successful Dutch planters from Brazil.
The Dutch their contribution were willing to make,
Since sugar to Europe they were equipped to take.
Experts in production the Dutch did provide,
In good times and bad the Dutch were by their side.

Plans for their future the Dutch had laid.
Handsome rewards they would later be paid.
Startling were the effects that sugar had,
Some were good and some were bad.
The demand for land was very, very high,
To their land, tobacco planters said a sad good-bye.
Some ended up in towns to start anew,
Many became buccaneers and pirates too.
Plantations replaced tobacco fields,
Gone were the days of a life of ease.

The plantation system created a new demand,
Labor had to be at the planters command.
For a hundred years the Spaniards had used,
Africans as slaves; Christianity was their excuse.
By 1650 the stage was set,
Slaves from Africa were the British to get.
Soon a new society did begin,
A society based on the color of the skin.

Wealth and power went hand in hand,
They were held by those who owned the land.
Those who worked, wealth to produce,
Were subjected daily to planters abuse.
Deliberate effort the system did make,
African culture from Africans to take.
England's economic future was firmly laid,
In a system for which West Africans paid.

In the Caribbean, new interest England did show,
In those islands where sugar did successfully grow.
The Dutch involvement was soon to end,
No longer on the Dutch the colonists could depend.
The needs of the colonists Britain would now provide,
On the Mother Country their future relied.
The entire Caribbean after 1650,
Became a base of European rivalry.

The Caribbean region had been transformed,
To a place where men fought, and where men farmed.
Spaniards and Frenchmen, British and Dutch,
Exploited the islands without a blush.
While from the islands great fortunes were made
Africa did suffer from continuous raids,
The Caribbean today is a reflection,
Of structures laid by the Sugar Revolution.

Lloyd E. Afflick

LEST WE FORGET

THE MICO COLLEGE

The Mico College, one of the most prestigious educational institutions in the West Indies today, was founded in 1836. The College has a most unusual but interesting beginning.

In 1670 Lady Mico left her estate valued at £1,000.00 to be used in one of two ways.
   a) To be given to a nephew of hers if he agreed to marry one of his six cousins.
   b) To be used to ransom Christian sailors who were captured by Barbary pirates off the coast of North Africa, if Stephen, Lady Mico's nephew refused to marry one of his six cousins.

Stephen refused to take his cousin as his bride and was therefore, not entitled to the money. Piracy ended in the Mediterranean before the money was used for ransom. The money was therefore not used to fulfill Lady Mico's will.

Between 1670 and 1830, the money had grown from £1,000.00 to £120,000.00. The Trustees had to decide what to do with such a large sum.

116

For many years various individuals had been working to end slavery in the British West Indies. For example, Granville Sharpe's efforts had led to the passage of a law in 1772 which made it illegal for anyone to own a slave in England. This law, The Mansfield Decision, led to the emancipation of 14,000 Blacks who had been taken to England by their masters.

Thomas Clarkson had, through his writings, awakened the consciences of people throughout England to the evils of slavery and the slave trade. William Wilberforce had spent his life working in Parliament to end the slave trade and finally slavery. In 1807 a bill passed ending the trade and just before the Bill to end slavery in 1833 was passed, Wilberforce died.

It should not be forgotten that changing economic circumstances in Britain and in the West indies contributed much to the decision to end slavery. This does not, however, detract from the fact that these men and many others had their hearts in the right place and did fight for emancipation.

With the ending of slavery in sight, the abolitionists began to give serious consideration to the social welfare of the freed slaves after emancipation. Legal freedom alone would in no way prepare the exslaves for life in a free society. It is important to note that Jamaica's slave population at the time of emancipation was just over 311,000.

Their social and economic needs were many. One of the greatest needs, however, was education. Ever since the religious revival of the late eighteenth century in England, missionaries had been working in the Caribbean. They were among the first people to attempt to educate the slaves. It was quite natural, therefore, that when the "Negro Education Grant" was made in 1833 the British Government would request the help of the missionaries and other church organizations in making provision for the education of the newly freed slaves.

It was not long before a very serious problem arose. With all their good intentions, the religious organizations were unable to provide the teachers to undertake the gigantic task. It was at this moment of crisis that a new leader of the abolition cause was found. He was none other than Thomas F. Buxton. Buxton had succeeded Wilberforce in Parliament. He was as dedicated as Wilberforce was to the cause of the improvement of the conditions of the former slaves. Since the struggle for emancipation was over, Buxton's major concern was the improvement of the social conditions of the newly freed people.

He had a particular interest in the improvement of education. As a result, Buxton argued convincingly that there could be no better cause to which the Lady Mico's fortune could be put than to the cause of educating the newly freed slaves. He emphasized that Lady Mico would be pleased that she was privileged to contribute to such a noble cause. Buxton prevailed and it was agreed that the Lady Mico's fortune was to be used for the education of the former slaves and their children forever.

About 1837 Mico schools were set up in Trinidad, Demerara (Guyana), Bahamas, and St.Lucia. Colleges for the training of teachers were established in Antigua and Jamaica. The Mico schools throughout the Caribbean gave place later to schools run by the Government.

Mico College—Jamaica

The Mico College in Jamaica has stood the test of time. Though it was founded as a teachers training institution and has continued to be, it has over the years gained a reputation for training leaders. Today, there are Mico graduates who are lawyers, doctors, ministers of religion, businessmen and women, professors, scientists, political leaders and of course class room teachers who are making their contribution in Jamaica and in numerous countries around the world.

For the greater part of its history, the Mico College was an institution for the training of male teachers. About 50 years ago the institution took in its first group of female students and has been co-educational ever since. It has been playing a leading role in the education of the people of Jamaica through its function as a teacher training institution for over 170 years.

Sir Thomas Fowell Buxton

Thomas F. Buxton is held in high esteem among all Miconians. The imposing clock tower of the original structure is named for him. He is also the patron of one of the Houses into which the college students are divided. Sir Thomas Buxton we salute thee! Mico and Miconians, continue to "DO IT WITH THY MIGHT"!

Jamaica

Jamaica is an island in the Caribbean Sea.
It is a land of great variety.
Its climate is beautiful all year round.
It is the land of the famous Reggae sound.

Plantains, bananas, yams and bread-fruit,
Sugar cane, coffee, pimento and citrus fruits
Throughout the island can be found,
They grow naturally from the fertile ground.

First inhabited by peaceful Indians,
Then came people from faraway lands.
The Spanish period was followed by British control,
They were both in search of Caribbean gold.

The plantation system held the fate
Of a new society which it was about to create.
Africans, Chinese, East Indians and Jews
Have lived in Jamaica, sharing cultural views.

If Jamaica you should ever visit,
It will be an experience you will never forget.
Its music, food and its people too,
Will forever become a part of you.

African Survivals in the Diaspora

Although everything possible was done during the days of slavery to destroy African traditional practices, much has survived to the present day. African <u>survivals</u> may be found to different degrees throughout the Americas.

The influence of traditional African culture may be found in the following areas:

- Music
- Speech
- Dance
- Communal Living
- Foods
- Crafts
- Games
- Medicine
- Oral Tradition

CHAPTER-7

African Contributions To Caribbean Culture

A. Continents, Cultures, Contact And Conflict

Long, long ago Europeans (Whites) lived in Europe; Asians lived in Asia, Native Americans lived in America and Africans (Blacks) lived in Africa.

About 550 years ago, change began in Europe. Change came because of the Renaissance. Europeans began to do things differently. Europeans began to think differently. Europeans began to sail the great oceans. Europeans tried to sail around Africa. Europeans met the people of West Africa.

The people of West Africa had their own way of life; they had their own culture. Africans had their own way of doing things. Africans had their own musical instruments. Africans played their instruments and danced differently.

Africans had many languages. They spoke differently. Africans had their own religions; They worshipped differently. African children loved to play games and listen to stories.

B. Continents, Cultures, Contact And Conflict
Native Americans Of The Caribbean

The Native Americans of the Caribbean were Arawaks and Caribs. They too had their own way of life. They had their own languages; they spoke differently. They had their own games; they played differently. They had their own religion; they worshipped differently. They had their own music; they danced differently.

Columbus sailed West ward from Spain. He hoped to reach the islands of the East Indies. Columbus ended up in the Caribbean. He met the Arawaks. He was welcomed by the Arawaks. He returned to the Caribbean with Spanish settlers. Columbus returned to the Caribbean three times. Each time he brought Spanish settlers.

The Spaniards wanted gold. The Spaniards wanted to grow crops on large farms or plantations. They enslaved the Arawaks. The Arawaks were forced to work in the mines and on the plantations. The Arawaks died out rapidly. They died from hard work. They died from ill-treatment. They died from strange diseases.

Later the English (British), French and Dutch came. They too established Plantations in the West Indies.

C. Capture, Transportation and Sale Of Africans
    The Triangular Trade

After the destruction of the Arawaks, European settlers needed workers. The Europeans went to Africa. They captured Africans and made them slaves. Africans were marched from the interior to the coast. Africans were sold at the coast. Africans lost their freedom. Africans became slaves.

Africans were put on ships. They did not take material things with them. All that they took were their ideas. They remembered the way they lived in Africa. They remembered how they worked; how they played; how they spoke; how they worshipped.

Many Africans died at sea on the way to the Caribbean. Some died of diseases; some died of ill-treatment. Some arrived in the Caribbean. The Africans were sold to plantation owners. The Africans became slaves on the plantations. The Africans provided labor to produce sugar.

Life On A West Indian Sugar Plantation

The plantation had many rules. Africans had to obey the plantation rules. They could not use their languages. They had to learn the language of the plantation masters. They mixed the language of their masters with African languages. They began new ways of speaking. British slaves mixed English with African languages. French slaves mixed French with African languages. Dutch slaves mixed Dutch with African languages.

African slaves told their children stories. Africans secretly practiced their religions. Their children played some African games. Africans continued to practice community living. They made drums and bells. They played their instruments and danced to the music. African ways were mixed with European ways. A new culture was born. It was the Caribbean culture.

African Survivals In Contemporary Caribbean Societies

Finally, the Africans were freed. Today, their descendants speak European languages and languages which developed from the mixing of the European languages and African languages. Their religion is a mixture of their master's religion and African religious practices. Their music and dance are very much like African traditional music and dance. They work together as their forefathers did in Africa. Children play games and listen to stories just as Africans used to do.

The people of the Caribbean today have much in common. They had masters from different countries of Europe but they came from the same cultural background and had the same experiences in the Caribbean. In spite of language differences, people of African heritage in the Caribbean today are one people. They have a common history and a common culture.

CHAPTER-8

African Survivals In The Caribbean

In 1503 the first Africans to be brought to the Americas to be enslaved were landed on Haiti (Hispaniola). In 1519 the first ship to cross the Atlantic bringing people from West Africa arrived. For the next 300 years ships continued to cross the Atlantic bringing people from all parts of West Africa to the Caribbean. French ships, British ships, Dutch ships, Portuguese ships, and many more were all involved.

Africans were brought, scattered among the islands where they and their descendants would work for the rest of their days. Given the circumstances under which they left their homeland, they were unable to bring material things with them. What they brought were elements of their culture or way of life.

In view of the fact that the planters' only interest was economic, they did everything they could to reduce proud Africans to mere bodies into which they hoped to implant foreign ideas and behaviors, hoping to make them more obedient and efficient workers.

This they did by passing laws prohibiting African cultural practices; punishing individuals who failed to comply with plantation rules, while promoting the 'virtues' of things European. In spite of the planters' efforts much that was African survived.

Some of the most commonly found elements of African culture found in the Caribbean today, include—folk tales, games, riddles, proverbs, art, music (the drum), and dance. Community cooperation was, until quite recently, a very important method of providing labor through group exchange of service (in place of cash payment). This practice was brought from Africa. The singing of work songs as workers labored in the fields was also African in origin. In spite of the high level of development of modern medicines and their availability, Caribbean people still believe in the curative powers of herbs (bush) and make extensive use of them. Certain hairstyles and methods of food preparation are also cultural practices which were brought from Africa.

The belief in the existence and power of spirits continue on some islands of the Caribbean. Certain African forms of worship continue in the Caribbean in a creolized form. Good examples are Pocomania in Jamaica, Voodoo / Vodun in Haiti, and Santeria in Cuba. While Christianity has become established as the major religion of Caribbean people, its practice in some places has been greatly influenced by certain African behaviors.

In spite of the above-mentioned survivals, there are very few other areas of Caribbean life where the African influence is as enduring as on Caribbean speech. African influence on speech varies from island to island depending on historical and demographic factors.

The attempt to suppress African languages and to promote their European counterparts over three hundred years of slavery only succeeded in producing speech patterns peculiar to the Caribbean. Today across the islands popularly referred to as the English speaking Caribbean, people speak a variety of dialects, which developed from the blending of English, African languages and various other languages depending on the individual island. The language combinations vary from island to island. As a result, no two islands have exactly the same dialect.

The study, which follows—<u>Historical Roots of Dialects Across the English Speaking Caribbean</u>—is an attempt to show how, after centuries of colonial control of the region, and the mixing of peoples from various cultural backgrounds new forms of speech emerged; speech commonly referred to as 'Caribbean Dialects'.

Historical Roots Of Dialect Across The English Speaking Caribbean

The dictionary defines dialect as any form of speech considered as deviant from a real or imagined standard; that is, speech peculiar to a district, region, class, community, or social or occupational group.

The dictionary's definition is certainly not true of dialects of the English speaking Caribbean. Caribbean dialects are forms of speech which grew out of a unique historical situation—European colonialism in the Caribbean.

Caribbean dialects are the results of the blending of English (and other European languages) with aspects of numerous African languages and languages from Asia over a long period. Though the vocabulary is largely English, African languages have contributed much in syntax (structure) and idioms (peculiarity of phraseology approved by usage.)

Caribbean dialects are the backbone of the ex-colonial cultures and are not limited by class, region, social or occupational group. They are today, the "languages" through which Caribbean people express themselves. They are the languages not only of day to day communication, but of music, drama, storytelling, and other forms of free expression.

Jamaica

Let us begin by taking a look at Jamaica. The island of Jamaica was first visited by Christopher Columbus on his second voyage in 1494. On arrival, he found a group of Native Americans (Arawaks) living there. The island was soon settled by Spaniards who began cattle rearing there.

At first, Native American labor was used but as the population declined. Africans were brought in to provide the labor needed. For nearly 150 years the island remained Spanish. In 1655, the island was captured by the British after slight resistance. The Spanish settlers left Jamaica for the larger Spanish islands—Hispaniola and Cuba. Before leaving, they freed their enslaved Africans who ran to the hills to become later, the Jamaica Maroons.

When the British arrived, they had to begin to develop a new colony. Buccaneering was the major activity after 1655 until the end of the 17th century. With the coming of the 18th century, the sugar plantation system which had been developing in the Eastern Caribbean using African labor for over 60 years was to become the basis of the Jamaican economy. The availability of large quantities of virgin lands in Jamaica, led to the migration of many sugar planters from the Eastern Caribbean where after 60 years the soil was losing its fertility.

It was not long before Jamaica developed into one of the Caribbean's major sugar producers. Capital and enterprise (entrepreneurship) were provided by the British. Labor was provided by Africans who were uprooted from their homeland in West Africa.

Unlike the British who came with one language only, the Africans who were brought to Jamaica (and the rest of the Caribbean) brought with them a vast number of cultural practices unknown to the British and literally dozens and dozens of languages. It was out of this unusual combination of languages and cultures in a new environment that Caribbean dialects in general and Jamaican dialect in particular were born.

Throughout this paper references will be made to authoritative sources; quotations will also be borrowed to support the thesis that Caribbean dialects are patterns of speech of societies created by European colonialism. Since a dialect results when two or more languages are mixed, and since the quality of the languages mixed will influence the nature of the dialect which results it is important to look closely at the quality of the language (English) which was used by "masters" with enslaved persons in a situation where profit from land and labor was the only concern.

Greenwood and Hamber in their book <u>Emancipation to Emigration,</u> give us a brief description of the English that was used on a plantation. "The language they (enslaved persons) heard in place of their tribal tongue was English in a mixture of <u>orders</u> and <u>abuse,</u> including plenty of <u>cursing.</u>" Plantation English then, was not the language of scholarship or even polite conversation. There was no Shakespeare, Tennyson, Wordsworth, Byron, or Keats; just enough English to get the job done.

To make a bad situation worse, in an attempt to destroy the African culture of the enslaved people, measures were taken which had far reaching effects on the speech patterns which developed on the plantations. Typical plantation practices included the separation of people of a given tribe. It was also a common practice to "season" enslaved persons on their arrival in the Caribbean.

Augier and Gordon in their book <u>Sources of West Indian History,</u> in commenting on the seasoning of slaves quote the words of a planter. "From the late Guinea sales, I have purchased altogether twenty boys and girls, from 10 to 13 years old. It is the practice on bringing them to the estate to distribute them in the huts of Creole Negroes under their direction and care, who are to feed them, train them to work and <u>teach them their new language.</u>"

Cater, Digby, and Murray in book 4 of the series, <u>The History of the West Indian People,</u> expand the point made above on seasoning. "As new slaves arrived they had to acquire the language their fellows used. It was not always possible to speak one of the several languages (brought from Africa) for on any plantation there may be found members of several tribes, Eboes, Yourbas, Ashanti, etc".

When one examines Michael Crowder's description of Nigeria in his book, <u>The Story of Nigeria</u> (1966), we get an impression of how complex the language spoken on a plantation must have been. He says, "Nigeria today (1966) is inhabited by a large number of tribal groups ranging in size from a few thousand to many millions, speaking between them <u>several hundred languages</u>"—NOTE: Nigeria is but one of many countries in West Africa."

What emerges from the above is the fact that the foundation of the language of any given British West Indian plantation was the result of the blending of contributions from the English language with elements of untold numbers of African languages.

The basic language combination of English/African which was the situation found in 18th century Jamaica was compounded by historical developments of the 19th century. The so-called slave trade finally ended in 1807. However, the demand for labor on the plantations continued. Since Africa was no longer a reliable source of labor, some Caribbean planters, (Jamaica included) turned to China and then India as suppliers of labor. Indian immigration which began in 1838 (when the enslaved people were finally freed) continued until 1917. Although there was not an immediate dramatic effect on Caribbean culture, by the ending of the immigration scheme (1917) the new-comers were definitely having an effect on Caribbean culture, language included.

The degree to which Caribbean islands experienced change in culture, depended on the individual island's demographic situation. This can be demonstrated by comparing Jamaica and Trinidad in 1834 and again in 1917.

In 1834, Jamaica's enslaved population numbered 311,070 and Trinidad's 20,660. As a result of emancipation, Indians and Chinese were brought to the Caribbean as indentured workers between 1838 and 1917; Jamaica received 33,000 while Trinidad received 134,000 (Augier and Gordon's <u>Making of the West Indies</u>). Although numbers are not given for the increase in black population of either island in 1917 when Indian immigration ended, it should not be difficult to see the dramatic effect immigration had on Trinidad, when one takes into consideration the size of Trinidad's population—while its impact on Jamaica was slight. Over 90% of Jamaica's population today is people of African descent.

TRINIDAD

The massive increases in the number of people arriving in Trinidad from the Far East (134,000) had far reaching effects on the island's culture; effects on food, religion, celebrations and quite naturally language. The matter becomes even more interesting when one examines Trinidad's demographic situation before the beginning of the period of immigration.

Although the island was visited by Spaniards as early as 1498 (Columbus' third voyage) and a settlement established as early as 1595, the island remained underdeveloped with a very small population until the end of the 18th century when French people sought refuge there during the French Revolution.

TRINIDAD AND TOBAGO

When Trinidad was ceded to Britain in 1803 therefore, it was an island with a very small community of French and Spanish speakers. This is made clear in a letter written to the Secretary of State for the Colonies by the British governor in Trinidad in 1841. (Sources of West Indian History, by Augier and Gordon). "Your Lordship will not fail to think this most essential when I tell you that two-thirds of the natives still speak exclusively either Spanish or French, and I conceive it absolutely necessary that people living under British rule and claiming the benefits of British subjects should be able to read the laws by which they are governed."

Edward Brathwaite's and Anthony Phillips' observations about Trinidad's culture at the time of the British takeover support the British governor's concern in his letter to the Colonial Secretary. Brathwaite and Phillips in the book, The People Who Came (book 3) state, "The majority of settlers were French (although Trinidad was technically Spanish, it had been practically taken over by French planters). This meant that in this island the majority spoke a language different from the people in power, their laws and custom different from British practice."

As late as 1841 then, Trinidad was a land of French and Spanish speakers. The date 1841 is most interesting since what seemed to be a major problem to the British governor was now to be compounded by a massive immigration of Chinese and Indian workers to Trinidad.

In spite of the Repatriation Clause in the Indians' contract which gave the right of a free return passage to India, Dr. Eric Williams, former Prime Minister of Trinidad, in his book Inward Hunger, states "One out of every three people in Trinidad in 1911 was an Indian." Today, about 40% of Trinidad's population is Indians.

Observations

The dialects of the English speaking Caribbean have all been influenced by the contributions of the English language and languages of Africa. In addition, the dialect as it is spoken on any given individual island today, is the result of contributions of various other factors; factors such as cultural contributions from other European and Asian countries during the formative years; influence of Caribbean non-English speaking neighbors; the impact of the media (radio, TV); exposure of islanders in foreign lands and the impact of tourism on the various island nations. It is important to note that what has happened over the years is that patters of speech have developed as a result of historical and demographic forces. Such patters of speech vary from island to island.

Each island's dialect is an ever-evolving aspect of its culture. A look at Haiti and the ABC islands will make this clear. In Haiti, a former French colony, what started out as a dialect is now a language in its own right, Haitian Creole. Papiamento, a language in the ABC islands (Aruba, Bon Aire, and Curacao) is another good example. What must have begun as a dialect is now the most commonly used language of the people. R.C. West and J.P. Augille state in their book, Middle America, It's Land and People, "The most common tongue in the Southern A.B.C. group is Papiamento, a trading language that developed as a remarkable mixture composed of words taken from Spanish, Portuguese, Dutch, English, and African languages."

The underlying principle, whether applied to the English speaking Caribbean, any other Caribbean society, or any society in any part of the world throughout history is human interaction leads to changes in both interacting parties. When this principle is applied to speech the result is usually a blending of aspects of the original languages.

One has to look no further than at the origins of the Romance Languages or the English language itself. In the book, <u>The Worlds, Past, and Present</u>: (H.B.J. Social Studies), the author states, "The Romans spread the Latin language to all parts of their empire. Latin became the basis of modern French, Spanish, and Italian. These Latin based languages are called the Romance Languages. It is quite safe to add, the fact that wherever the Romans went their language was blended with the vernacular or language of the people who occupied the region. Latin also contributed many words to English, German, and other European languages that are not Romance Languages."

English itself, which was a major contributor to Caribbean dialects, was the result of languages which preceded it and out of which English developed. As Robert C. Pooley (et. al.) states in the book, <u>England: In Literature,</u> "The history of English literature begins roughly 1600 years ago when the Roman legion abandoned the province of Britain and left the native Celts a prey to conquest by Ango-Saxon tribes from the north of Europe." The English language experienced further development as a result of the Norman French and German influences later.

What makes Caribbean dialects different from the European counterparts is the fact that a European language developed as a result of the contributions of a series of invasions of a particular territory and its original inhabitants. While, in the case of the Caribbean, new languages and dialects developed as a result of the meeting and interacting of various peoples from various cultural backgrounds in a foreign environment, the Caribbean, with the express purpose of the exploitation of human and natural resources for profit which would later be repatriated to lands across the seas, the so-called mother countries. In the case of the English-speaking Caribbean, the mother country was England.

Caribbean dialects then, are forms of speech with their roots firmly grounded in Caribbean history. As Greenwood and Hamber state in their book <u>Emancipation to Emigration</u>, "Among the slaves there developed a patois, a mixture of English, French, Indian, African (tribal and Creole). After generations, this had a right to be called a language with its own words and grammar. However, in the period of slavery the West Indian culture forms lacked self confidence and could not break the feeling of being neither one nor the other."

Since emancipation (1838), dialects have become more and more complex. Improvements in transportation and communication have enhanced cultural contact. This in turn has had its effect on speech patterns across the Caribbean. Language is dynamic, Caribbean dialects therefore will continue to change with time.

Whatever changes might take place, the dialects are here to stay. They are expressions of the souls of Caribbean people. On any given island, the dialect transcends racial, religious, and class barriers. An island's dialect is definitely an expression of the island's nationality. It is one of those things which bind a group of people together, setting them apart as a specific group. As mentioned earlier, it is the language of poetry and song; the language of a people's story, of good times and bad times, a story which only Caribbean people truly understand.

Caribbean Dialect

In addition to the major contributors (English and African Languages) to the Caribbean dialect, there are other cultural influences which need to be considered. These will vary from island to island, based on the history of individual islands. Barbados is the only island, which remained a British colony throughout its colonial period.

Caribbean dialect is not a form of speech peculiar to a district, region, class, community, social or occupational group (of the larger society). It is a form of speech which grew out of a unique historical circumstance-European (British) colonialism in the Caribbean.

It is the result of the blending of the English language with aspects of numerous African languages over 300 years, and languages of other countries. Though the vocabulary is largely English, African languages have contributed much in syntax (structure) and idioms (peculiarity of phraseology approved by usage).

Linstid Markit

"Carry Mi Ackee go A Linstid Markit
Nat a quatty Wut Sell.
Carry Mi ackee go a Linstid Markit
Nat a quatty wut sell.

Chorus

Lawd, Wat a Nite, Nat a Bite
Wat a Satiday Nite!
Lawd wat a nite, Nat a bite
Wat a Satiday nite!

Everybady come feel up, Feel up
Nat a quatty wut sell
Everybady come feel up, Feel up
Nat a quatty wut sell

Mek Mi bawl it out ackee, ackee.
Red an pritty dem tan.
Lady buy yu Sundiy manin brekfas.
Rice and ackee nyam gran.

All di pickney dem linga. Linga.
A weh dem Muma go bring.
All di pickney dem linga. Linga.
A weh dem Muma go bring."

(Folk Songs of Jamaica, Tom Murray)

Jamaica
(And Other English Speaking Caribbean Islands)
The Post Emancipation Period

On August 1, 1838 all the enslaved people throughout the English speaking Caribbean were granted their freedom. No preparation was made for their social or economic well being.

The islands were to experience a period of great difficulty. The planter class managed to survive by seeking out new sources of labor for their plantations. First, China was tried as a source from which to recruit indentured workers. The scheme did not prove to be a success. Then Madeira and India were tried as sources of labor. It was the scheme of Indian immigration which rescued the plantations from total disaster; especially in Jamaica and the newly acquired Trinidad and Guiana.

While the planter class was taking care of its own economic interests, the newly freed people were left to their own devices. Government neglect, unavailability of land and dire poverty led to protests and social uprisings, the most serious of which took place in Jamaica and came to be known as the Morant Bay Rebellion (1865). As a result of this uprising Jamaica lost its Assembly System of government and become a crown colony

Economic hardship persisted throughout the Caribbean. As time went by, people returned to the soil and began to produce various crops for which they could find markets abroad. For example, St Vincent began to produce arrowroot; Grenada, nutneg; Trinidad, coconut and cocoa.

Jamaica became the producer of bananas by chance. The newly freed people had been producing crops such as yams, plantains and bananas to feed themselves.

In the 1870's an American, one Captain Baker, visited Jamaica and on his return voyage to the U.S.A. took a load of bananas to see if he could find a market in the U.S.A. His experiment was a great success, and so, the Jamaica banana industry was born. Small farmers now had a crop on which they could depend. Coconuts too would become an important economic item.

CHAPTER-9

The French in the Caribbean

Spain's chief enemies in the Caribbean were the British and French. Unlike the Dutch whose interest was limited to trade, the British and French were interested in establishing empires of their own.

In 1625, a group of Frenchmen landed on St. Kitts after being attacked at sea by the Spaniards. The British, who had established a colony on the island in 1624, welcomed the French, hoping to benefit from joint-defense. The French colony which was established on St. Kitts lasted for just a short time however.

French colonization began in earnest in 163 5 when a group of settlers organized by businessmen and the French government settled Martinique and Guadeloupe. By the middle of the eighteenth century, France exercised great influence over the islands of the Lesser Antilles. In addition to Martinique and Guadeloupe, France claimed St. Vincent, Tobago, Grenada, and Dominica. Both St. Lucia and Grenada were settled in 1648.

The struggle for dominance in the Caribbean whether for economic or strategic reasons, led to the constant shifting of islands from one European power to the other, as they were constantly being used as pawns to settle Europeans disputes.

The French position in the Caribbean was gradually weakened however, while the British position was strengthened by Treaties which ended major European conflicts. The Treaty of Paris (1763), The Treaty of Versailles (1783), and The Treaty of Vienna played a very important part in shifting the balance of power in the Caribbean in Britain's favor.

After 1814 France was left with no more than Martinique and Guadeloupe in the Eastern Caribbean. All the other islands, which were owned by France, became British possessions.

Haiti

Haiti, the western third of the island of Hispaniola started out as a buccaneer colony. During the first half of the 17th century a group of buccaneers established a base on Tortuga Island off the north-western shores of Hispaniola. The colony was made up of British, French and Dutch men.

In 1654, a French governor D'Ogeron established a French colony on Hispaniola at Port Marogot. The following year (1655) Jamaica was captured from the Spaniards by the British. Shortly after, British buccaneers moved to Jamaica, leaving Tortuga to the French.

Within a hundred years, Haiti grew to be the richest colony in the Americas. In 1791 the Haitian slaves revolted. By 1803 they were victorious. Haiti declared its independence in 1804. After 1804 France's colonial strength in the Caribbean was reduced to Martinique and Guadeloupe only.

Although French colonial interest in the Caribbean was reduced to two small islands after 1804, French cultural influence can still be felt throughout the region.

Haiti-Where It All Began

The islands between North and South America are called the Islands of the Caribbean or the West Indies. Five hundred years ago they were the homelands of Native American peoples called Arawaks and Caribs.

The larger islands, Jamaica, Cuba, Puerto Rico and Hispaniola, in addition to the Bahamas were inhabited by Arawaks.

The Arawaks gave names to the islands they occupied. Guanahani was the island where Columbus first landed. It was renamed San Salvador by Columbus. Xaymaca, land of wood and water was renamed Jamaica. Haiti, land of high mountains was renamed Hispaniola.

Jamaica, Cuba and Puerto Rico were settled from Haiti. Haiti is very important in New World history.

1. It was the first place in the New World on which a European village, Isabella was made.

2. Santo Domingo, the oldest city in the New World was established on Haiti.

3. The use of Native Americans by Europeans, Spaniards, as workers in mines and on plantations began on Haiti.

4. The first Africans to be brought to the New World to work in mines and on plantations were brought to Haiti.

5. Many of the plants used for food in the New World, were brought from the Old World and were first grown on the island of Haiti. Good examples are grapes, oranges, figs, lemons, rice, bananas, and sugarcane.

6. Many animals were also brought from the Old World to the New World and were first reared on the island of Haiti—cattle, pigs, sheep, goats, chickens, mules, and donkeys are good examples.

Haiti was where people of the Old World first lived among people of the New. Haiti was where it all began.

Haiti

[This island was named 'Haiti' by its first people-the Arawaks. The name Haiti means-land of high mountains.]

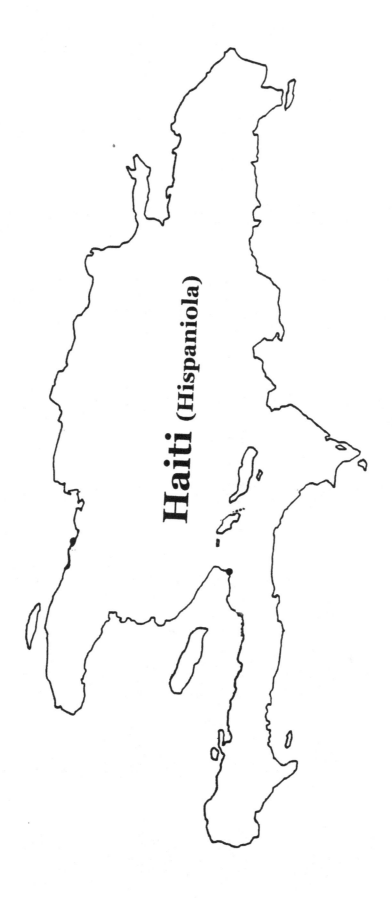

[The island was re-named-Hispaniola by Christopher Columbus.]

Lloyd E. Afflick

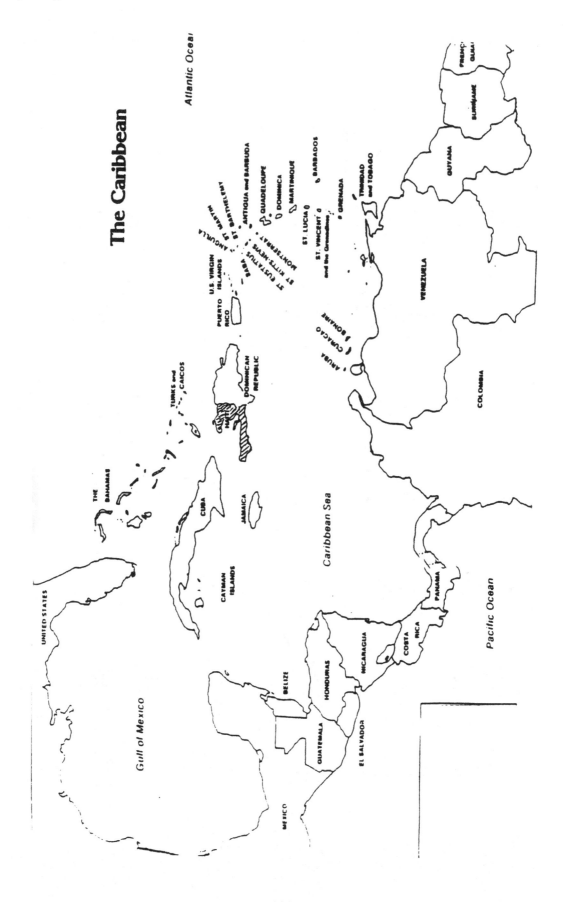

The Caribbean

146

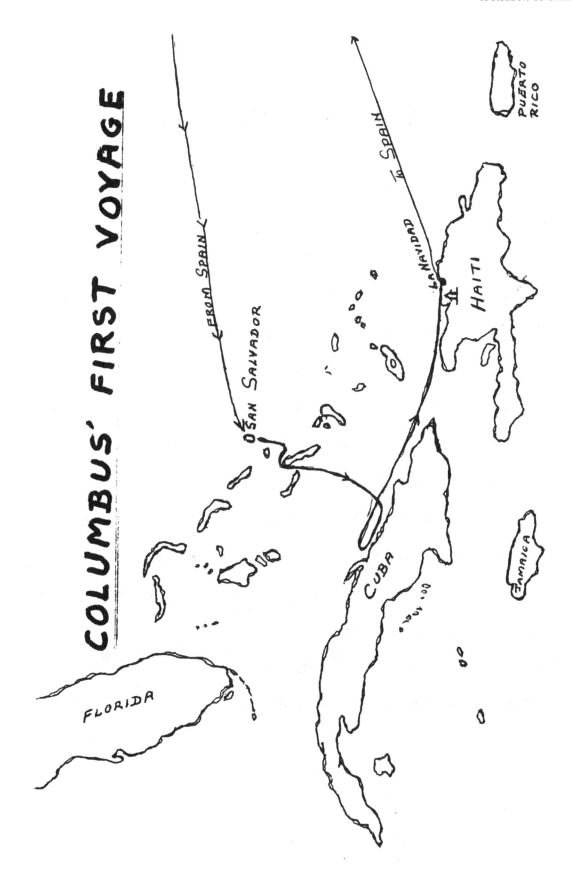

The Coming of the French

The first French men settled on the island of Tortuga.

They were buccaneers.

They made their living by hunting wild animals.

In 1654, French people settled on the western part of the island of Haiti (Hispaniola).

They named that part of the island St. Domingue.

They made large plantations (farms) of sugarcane.

The French also grew cotton, coffee, cocoa, and citrus fruits.

They brought African people to do the work on the plantations.

The African people were enslaved.

The Africans worked for many years as slaves.

The Africans wanted to be free, and so they fought against the French.

The African people gained their freedom (independence) from France on January 1, 1804.

They renamed their part of the island Haiti.

The people of Haiti became known as Haitians.

Haitians are a proud, hard-working group of people.

THE COMING OF FRENCH

ST. DOMINGUE

(HAITI)

PORT MARGOT

CAP FRANCAIS

[France settled the western part of the island in 1654. the French named it St. Domingue. By 1789 St. Domingue had become the richest colony in the Americas by producing coffee, sugar and cotton. Enslaved Africans did the work on the plantations.]

[In 1804 St. Domingue was renamed Haiti]

A Reason To Smile

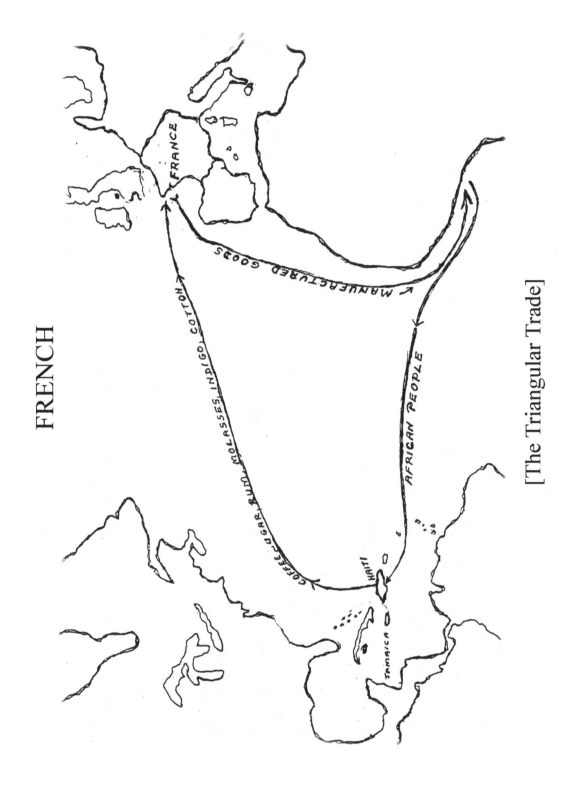

FRENCH

[The Triangular Trade]

Interesting Facts About Haiti

Toussaint L'Overture rose from slavery to become one of the great military Generals of all time.

1. Haiti was the only slave society to have had a successful slave revolt.

2. Simon Bolivar visited Haiti then returned to Venezuela to lead the liberation of South America. He gained inspiration from the Haitian people.

3. Frederick Douglass, the famous African American abolitionist spent his last working years as American ambassador to Haiti.

4. The City of Chicago was founded by Jean Baptiste Du Sable, a sea-captain and explorer from Haiti.

5. In 1779, five hundred and forty-five Haitians fought in Savannah, Georgia, in support of the American Patriots who were fighting for their freedom from Britain.

6. Many historians argue that Napoleon's decision to sell Louisiana to the U.S.A. in 1803 was the result of frustration caused by the defeat of the French forces in Haiti in 1802.

7. Henry Christophe who ruled northern Haiti (1806-18200 served in the volunteer army which fought in Georgia in 1797.

8. Among the writers of international repute who contributed to the Harlem Renaissance was Jean Price Mars from Haiti.

9. Haitian art has gained recognition worldwide. The Haitian people have for many years been producers of things of beauty in spite of adversity.

10. Haiti has given to the world another language.

HAITI'S GIFT TO THE U.S.A.

The success of the Haitian colony caused Napoleon to give thought to building an empire in Louisiana. Haiti would supply Louisiana with its economic needs.

Boukman, a Jamaican maroon, invited plantation slaves to the mountains and trained them in the meaning of freedom. At a given signal they would rise up and fight for their freedom. Toussaint should be the leader of the Revolution.

The Haitian Revolution was timed to begin at the same time as the French Revolution. The Haitian slaves were meeting with great success when the leaders of the French forces invited Toussaint to go aboard ship to talk "peace". They sailed away with him to France where he died in a messy dungeon.

Dessalines took over command of the Haitian forces, slaves and maroons, and led them to victory. Haiti declared its independence from France on January 1, 1804.

At the very time of France's defeat, the President of the United States had sent some ambassadors to France to negotiate the purchase of a small piece of land at the mouth of the Mississippi to build a harbor from which to sail up the river.

Having lost Haiti, Napoleon was so disappointed and broken-hearted that he changed his mind about building his New World Empire in Louisiana. When the discussions began about the purchase of the land at the mouth of the Mississippi, Napoleon shocked the Americans. "Give me fifteen million dollars and take Louisiana". Without getting permission from the President they closed the deal. The U.S.A. had just doubled its size for fifteen million dollars.

This purchase made what was later known as the Western Expansion to begin. All that land in the central portion of North America, Louisiana, became U.S.A. territory because of the victory of the Haitian people over France.

It is, therefore, possible to argue that Louisiana was a gift from the Haitian people to the United States of America.

The Louisiana Purchase

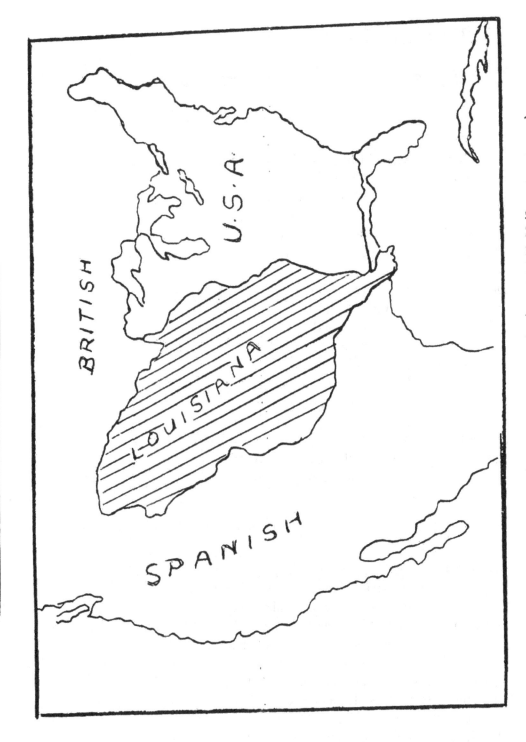

Louisiana was purchased from France in 1803 for $15,000,000.00 (3 cents per acre)

Let Freedom Ring!!
A Tribute to the Haitian People

Napoleon Bonaparte, Military genius was he,
Greater than Alexander he aspired to be.
Great victories in Europe this Frenchman did win,
He left his mark wherever he'd been.
The conflict in France was for liberty,
The people were tired of the aristocracy.

Domestic problems as you will see
Were soon to be felt internationally.
Italy and England, Portugal and Spain
Felt the effects of Napoleon's reign.
The Sugar colony of Haiti he had to win
If his new world empire he should being.

A fleet was sent under General LeClerc,
Plantation slaves to put back to work.
The French fleet arrived after many weeks passed.
The stage was set for a show down at last.
Masters or slaves, who would it be?
Which side would win the victory?

For France's glory LeClerc did attack,
The freedom of slaves he had to take back.
An invitation was extended by General LeClerc.
Toussaint accepted hoping peace would work.
Toussaint was arrested and sent to France.
Dessalines took charge and continue the advance.

Toussaint, Dessalines and Henry Christophe
Great me of Haiti, these leaders three.
Napoleon, LeClerc and Roch-ambeau
Did all that French generals usually do.
Yet the quest for freedom they could not stop,
The people of Haiti had had enough.

The might of Europe the French did defeat.
Napoleon's France the Haitian's did beat.
Haiti was one of the countries three,
With new governments revolutionary.
Haiti's success was bound to be
One of history's great victories.

The course of history the Haitians did change
This was certainly not to France's advantage.
Napoleon abandoned his new world empire.
He decided to sell his cherished Louisiana.
Whenever you think of the U.S. of A.
Remember the roll the Haitians did play.

Hail to thee, dear people of Haiti!
We appreciate the lesson we learnt from three.
Poverty and terror you now endure
A brighter tomorrow awaits you for sure.
Unite and recapture the freedom you won
Believe it! Achieve it! You certainly can!

The President Speaks

My name is Augustus Reid,
I am here to interview President Aristide.

What do you see as your major task now that you are back in office?
I am President Aristide;
I have six million mouths to feed.

How will you insure that Haiti remains democratic?
I am President Aristide;
The people's council I will heed.

How will Haiti over-come so many problems?
I am President Aristide
For me to succeed,
International goodwill I will need.

The future of Haiti rests with the children.
What are your plans for them?
I am President Aristide.
Haitian children must learn to write and read.

Your country's survival will depend on its ability to feed itself.
What are your plans for agriculture?
I am President Aristide
We urgently need efficient tools and a variety of seeds.

There are great social divisions in Haiti.
What will you do to encourage togetherness?
That's a very good question indeed.
Each Haitian will daily do a good deed

Mr. President do you think you can accomplish
All that is to be done by yourself?
I am President Aristide!
Together we will work and succeed; my role is to lead.

Mr. President will you please,
Briefly outline your developmental strategy.
That's another good question you've asked of me.
We will go from poverty to plenty with dignity.

Mr. President can you imagine your people ever
Again enduring such pain?
Never, never, never again.
Mr. Reid, let me repeat it again.
Never, never, never, never again*!*

Dutch Influence in the Caribbean

The Dutch emerged from the Middle Ages with the reputation of being one of Europe's leading nations in fishing and industry. By the 15th century they were among the leading trading people in Europe.

The Dutch were among the first people to challenge Spain's power in the New World. They arrived in the early seventeenth century in search of salt. Salt was important because it was used to preserve fish. Salt was found in great quantities at the Araya Lagoon in Venezuela. At the beginning of the seventeenth century, over 120 ships visited the Caribbean to load salt for the Dutch fishing industry each year.

On the journey from Europe to the Caribbean, the salt ships transported trade goods such as cloth, tools, and other plantation supplies to be sold to the Spanish settlers. On the return voyage, salt ships transported Caribbean products such as sugar, tobacco and hides.

Between 1630 and 1640 the Dutch established trading bases on Curacao, and Bonaire, islands not suitable for agricultural purposes.

Although the Dutch did not develop plantations of their own, they played a very vital role in the plantation economy of the British and French in the Caribbean. The Dutch provided plantation supplies, expertise in the growing and making of sugar, transportation to take agricultural produce back to Europe, and financial assistance (loans) to planters when they fell on hard times.

Today Dutch influence can still be felt on the islands which were used as trading bases. The greatest reminder of their presence in the Caribbean is the Dutch language. In addition to Dutch, Papiamento, a language which developed out of the blending of Dutch, English, Spanish, Portuguese and African languages can be found on Aruba, Bonaire and Curacao.

Languages Across the Caribbean

Spanish
Cuba
Puerto Rico
Dominican Republic

French
Martinique
Guadeloupe
Haiti (French. Haitian Creole)

Dutch, Papiamento. English
Aruba
Bonaire
Curacao

English
Trinidad and Tobago
Virgin Islands
Anguilla
Antigua
Dominica
St. Lucia
Barbados
St. Vincent
Grenada
Bahamas
Jamaica
Turks and Caicos
Cayman Islands

History of The Americas

The Caribbean
Conquest, Colonialism, Commerce, Culture

Important Dates:

1492, August 3: Columbus sailed from Spain

1492, October 12: Columbus arrived in the Bahamas

1492, December: Columbus visited Haiti

1493: Columbus returned to Haiti with 1500 settlers

1494: Treaty of Tordesillas signed

1502: First Africans brought to Haiti (Caribbean)

1508: Balboa visited Panama/1513 de Leon visited Florida

1518: First ship sailed directly from Africa to the Caribbean with people to be enslaved

1519: Hernando Cortez said from Cuba to Conquer Mexico

1535: Pizarro sailed to Peru to begin the conquest of the Inca Empire.

1492-1624: Spain exercised complete control over the Caribbean

1624: First British settlement established on St. Kitts.

1625: French settlers joined the British on St. Kitts.

16 20 & 1630's; Nevis, Antigua, Montserrat, Barbados settled by the British; Martinique and Guadeloupe settled by the French.

1640 (about): Buccaneer colony formed on Tortuga off the North Coast of Haiti.

1654: French Government sent settlers to settle (San Domingue) Haiti.

1655: Jamaica captured from Spain by the British

1670: Spain recognized Britain's right to keep Jamaica (Treaty of Madrid)

1697: Spain recognized France's right to keep San Domingue (Treaty of Ryswick)

1700-1800: The Caribbean was the leading producer of wealth (sugar plantation system) in the Americas.

1780's: Haiti (San Domingue) the richest colony in the world, supplied half of Europe with coffee, sugar and cotton.

1791: Enslaved Africans in Haiti revolted against France.

1804: Haiti became an independent nation

1815: Trinidad ceded to Britain

1807: Britain outlawed the slave—trade

1834: Britain passed law to end slavery in the English speaking Caribbean.

1838: Slavery ended in English speaking Caribbean

1840's: Chinese/Indian immigration schemes began

1865: Morant Bay Rebellion in Jamaica

1902: Cuba became an independent country

1952 Puerto Rico became commonwealth of the U.S.A.

1917: Indian immigration scheme ended.

1962: Jamaica became independent, beginning the age of independence in the English speaking Caribbean

Caribbean Economy Today

Farming, mining, manufacturing, food processing, fishing, tourism.

CHAPTER-10

THE AFRICAN AMERICANS

The American Story
The Role of Africans in the Growth and Development of the United
States of America.

Enslavement of Africans on Cotton Plantations (U.S.A.)

Caribbean colonial development was soon to be joined by developments in North America. Virginia, as it came to be called, began as a tobacco producer. In fact, it was Virginia's success in tobacco production which forced the British in the Eastern Caribbean to find a new export crop—sugar. Caribbean territories could not compete against Virginia's tobacco production.

The first British colony, Virginia, was established in 1607. Its economy was based on the production of rice, sugar, indigo and tobacco. In its earliest period, labor was provided by members of the planter's family and indentured servants from England.

In 1619, the first group of Africans landed in Virginia. They were not slaves. They joined the ranks of British indentured servants. They did the same type of work and worked under conditions similar to those of white indentured workers. At the end of their indenture, they were freed. They had the right to become independent proprietors, like their former employers.

The system of indenture lasted for about 40 years. Later, Africans who were brought to North America were made slaves. Slaves differed from indentured servants in that they had no rights as people. They were classified as property. They could be bought, sold or even given away. Their children and grandchildren were also the master's property.

The growing demand for tobacco, led to a demand for labor. More and more Africans were brought to North America and enslaved. Increase in the number of Africans led to the decision to end the indentured system and to develop an economy based on slave labor only.

As time passed, cotton became the major plantation crop. There was a great demand for cotton. As much as the southern plantation owners could produce, British textile manufacturers could buy. Demand for labor stimulated the development of an organized trade in African people.

The Middle Passage was the name given to the second leg of the journey taken by a slave ship (i.e., the passage from Africa to the Americas).

On the Middle Passage, African people were horribly treated. Ships were usually overcrowded. Little or no provision was made for sanitation. At times, Africans died by the hundreds on a single voyage because of overcrowding, poor nutrition, ill treatment, diseases and occasional suicide. Africans, who survived the Middle Passage, were sold to planters who enslaved them.

Slaves were classified according to the work they had to do. Those who worked in the Great House, taking care of the master's daily needs were called house slaves. Those who performed the technical services such as carpenters, masons, wheel-wrights, mechanics, sailors, etc. were called skilled slaves. Those who worked in the fields, cleaning the land, planting the crops, harvesting the crops were called field slaves.

Field slaves were the most important group. They were the ones who made the plantation economy possible. The wealth generated by the southern plantations was the result of the work done by field slaves. Although they worked the hardest, they were least trusted and most often punished.

Although much was done to destroy their African traditions, enslaved Africans managed to preserve and pass on much of their African cultural practices.

By the middle of the 18th century, cotton had become the chief crop in the South. In 1793, Eli Whitney's cotton gin revolutionized cotton production. The machine cleaned as much cotton in a given time as fifty persons (slaves) could. As a result, more and more land was put under cotton. More Africans were brought in and enslaved.

Harsh conditions under slavery and the growing influence of the abolitionists, led to increased slave resistance. Slaves planned revolts, destroyed crops, refused to work, and ran away (Underground Railroad).

By the 1820's it was clear that the economic future of the South would depend on cotton. The cotton plantation system depended on slavery. As the nation grew and more and more land became available in (Especially after the Louisiana Purchase.) the West for development, the rift between the North and the South grew intensely over the question of slavery.

Finally, there was open confrontation between the North and South over the question of the development of slavery in the West. When the South failed to get its way it threatened to secede from the Union. President Abraham Lincoln refused to preside over the division of the nation. As a result there was the outbreak of the Civil War.

The Making of a People

The journey ended, a new life began,
It was life on a Southern Plantation.
The African was apprenticed to a seasoned slave,
Whose duty it was to teach the plantation ways.
African names and languages had to go,
So European customs would have a chance to grow.

Traditional ranks and social class
Were simply things of the African past.
Rules of the plantation the planters gave,
Before them all were simply African slaves.
The hours of labor the planters set,
Rewards for labor were the planters to get.

Children and grandchildren were 'property' too,
Trained early in life to 'do what their parents do'.
And just in case the planter had the whim,
He was free to sell hard-working Jim.
Jim might be his mother's special prize,
Little did it matter in his master's eyes.

Conditions were worse at picking time,
The planters wanted to earn every single dime.
Labor was hard, punishment severe,
Money was all about which the master cared.
Some picked cotton, some bundles did make,
Some to the gin, the cotton did take.

Some at the gin working day and night,
Constantly dreaming of freedom's delight.
Fortunes from plantations the planters made,
Never for their labor were the Africans paid.
Night after night they would go to sleep,
Thinking of Africa they would frequently weep.

In such desolation they sometimes clung to hope,
That was the feeling which helped them to cope.

With backs a-bleeding and hearts in pain,
They thought of tomorrow and the plantation again.
"An end to this misery I cannot see,
Good God Almighty can't you help me?"

And so it was for over two hundred years,
Great wealth was made from blood, sweat, and tears.
Battered and bruised and left for dead,
A culture rebounded triumphantly instead.
Capture, enslavement and all the terrible wrong,
Simply succeeded in making a people **strong!**

The Civil War and After

For four long years (1861-1865) the nation was engaged in the Civil War. The conflict ended in 1865 with the defeat of the South. The years which followed were years during which the rebuilding of the nation was a major concern. The period of rebuilding came to be called—The Reconstruction Period. During Reconstruction the nation experienced social, economic, and political changes.

The political changes were of great importance. It was during Reconstruction that the 13th, 14th, and 15th Amendments were passed. The passage of these amendments ended slavery; made the newly freed persons citizens and granted them voting rights. Social services including education became a reality for the newly freed persons. For 10 long years progress was made. It all came to an end with the 1877 Compromise which solved the problem created when the election of 1876 ended with no clear winner for the office of President.

The 1877 Compromise ended the period of African American advancement. A new period began. It was a period of segregation, discrimination and intimidation for African Americans. The period was called "The Jim Crow" period.

Segregation and discrimination were legalized in 1896 when the Supreme Court handed down its ruling in the Plessey vs. Ferguson case. The exploitation of African Americans continued through to the 20th century. Sharecropping became one of the major economic outlets for African American labor.

African Americans could do very little about what was happening to them since they were unable to influence the political process. The poll tax, grandfather clause, and literacy test disqualified them from political participation. However, individuals worked hard to change the system. Good examples of African American leaders of the time were Booker T. Washington, Dr. W.E. B. DuBois, Marcus Garvey and Ida B. Wells.

The first World War provided an opportunity for young African American soldiers to be exposed to a different kind of life overseas. After the war, they were unwilling to accept the life they knew before the war, at home.

Opportunities in the North and economic depression in the South resulted in a large-scale movement of African Americans to northern cities.

Harlem became home to many African Americans. During the 1920s, a new mood swept through Harlem. African Americans expressed their creative genius through writing, art, sculpture, drama, music and dance. This was the period that came to be known as The Harlem Renaissance. Not until the Great Depression (1929-1933) did the Renaissance come to an end.

African Americans continued to struggle through the difficult years of the 1920s. Socially, economically and politically, limitations were placed in their way.

The Second World War was an event that provided opportunities for some African Americans. As was the case with the War of Independence, the Spanish American War, and the Civil War, African Americans again distinguished themselves in all areas in which they were assigned, including the Air Force.

In spite of their brilliant performance in the Second World War, African Americans had to endure much in the way of segregation and discrimination. However, many realized that they were ambassadors of the African American community and used the opportunity to prove that they were as good as any other group in the U.S.A.

In spite of the unfortunate experiences in the military, positive things did happen. Both President Eisenhower and President Truman took steps to begin to break down barriers that had been created during the Jim Crow era.

While things were happening to bring about change at the national level, African Americans were making efforts on their own, to bring equal opportunity for all in the society. A. Philip Randolph planned the first large-scale march on Washington in 1941, to protest discriminatory practices in employment, and Mary McLeod Bethune made her mark on education.

African American protests and daily demands on the system by individuals and groups (e.g. N.A.A.C.P.) led to gradual change. In 1954, a landmark case was won—Brown vs. Board of Education. It was this case which brought an end to legal segregation in education.

It was in 1955, one year after the Supreme Court's decision in Brown vs. Board of Education, which ended legal segregation in education that Rosa Parks took her stand against segregation on public transportation.

This event brought Dr. Martin Luther King to the fore front as leader of the African American community. It marked the beginning of a new chapter in the struggle for Civil Rights. The years from 1955-1964 were years of continuous pressures, struggles, and demands for Civil Rights. In 1964, a Civil Rights Act was passed and the following year a Voting Rights Act was also passed.

The last 50 years have been years during which all groups in the U.S.A. should have been enjoying equal rights. The real test however, is not in the laws passed to bring about change, but the degree to which the laws have been implemented. To what degree have the barriers (social, economic, and political) placed between peoples by the Jim Crow era been replaced by social, economic and political practices which are designed to bring about equality of opportunity for all the people of the nation? The answer to this question is the true measure of the Civil Rights movement.

Journey to the Cross Roads

The pressures of Europe they could take no more,
So the first settlers sailed for America's shore.
Starvation and disease took many lives,
The Indians taught them how to survive.
Then a good education simply meant,
Learning to master the environment.

As the years passed and the colonies grew,
The colonist denied all other cultural views.
Indian cultures they soon debased,
Indians were soon to be seen as an inferior race.
Africans were brought from the orient,
They were treated with utter contempt.

Early schools had their part to play,
To ensure that society remained that way.
The Indians they tried to Christianize,
The aim was to make them "civilized".
Africans were treated as property,
Outside the bounds of society.

So the American society began,
It was the plan of the Europeans.
Africans and Indians had much to share
But of such cultures, the settlers would not hear.
And so the races grew further apart,
It was the settlers plan from the start.

After a century and a half of continuous growth,
The colonists realized their "colonial worth".
Britain its power insisted to maintain
The colonists had had enough of King George's reign,
And so their Revolution they decided to begin,
A war the colonists were destined to win.

The Revolution over, Independence won,
The leaders' aim was to create a nation.

The War of 1812 played an important part,
In getting America off to a new start.
Then was born American nationalism,
Giving rise to a new patriotism.

Non-whites the system chose to exclude,
Preferring to continue the traditional feud.
The Indians were a major national problem,
The question was "how to get rid of them".
Slavery took on a new dimension,
With Eli Whitney's new invention.

America's major industrial age,
Was still at its very early stage.
Indian lands were a special attraction.
Southerners dreamt of expanding plantations.
Day after day new laws were passed
To ensure the Blacks remained a permanent slave class.

To a "different school" each group daily would go,
Seeds of the future, education would sow
Leaders and owners, whites were trained to be,
The virtues of White culture they hoped the Indians would see.
Blacks were taught to accept with grace
Their sub-human position; they should stay in their place.

Emphasis was placed on assimilation,
With the arrival of the mid-century Europeans.
European ways they were encouraged to abandon
In order to become true Americans.
Their American dream very early began,
Unlike the Indians and the Africans.

Sectional differences were coming to a head,
Rather than change, the South planned to secede instead.
More and more there were slave unrests,
Brutal treatment the slaves did utterly detest.
The gift of freedom which nature bestowed
Was soon to be found on the Underground Railroad

Thousands and thousands to the North did run
Seeking the promised American freedom.
Churches and barns were favorite stations,
The bravest conductor was Harriet Tubman.
Day by day the regions drifted apart
The stage was being set for the Civil War to start.

When finally the South could not have its way,
In the Union, no longer, it would willingly stay.
Lincoln would maintain the Union at all cost,
He would not preside over a Southern loss.
And so it was that the Civil War began,
The War which led to emancipation.

Imagine dear reader the way we felt!
We thanked God Almighty for deliverance sent.
With joy in our hearts we greeted each day,
Hoping that feeling forever would stay.
A society divided now had its chance,
For the first time in history, to unite at last!

Finally after centuries, this country had its chance,
As one people together, to advance at last.
Yes!! America had its chance!!

Compromise

You give a little, I give a little,
That's the nature of compromise.
You give a little; I give a little,
That's how to solve it if you are wise.
'Give and take at times friends make
Ambitions are sacrificed for peace sweet sake.

Such agreements are good and noble
When they are not against another person.
American history clearly demonstrates,
The ill-effects of 'give and take'.
The North and the South did compromise
At the tragic expense of African lives.

In 1787 the leaders had to agree
On the future position of slavery.
On representation all southerners did agree,
"Slaves are men as much as we".
This view point the northerners refused to see,
To Northerners; all slaves were simply property.

On the question of taxes Northerners did agree,
Slaves were men as all could see.
"No", argued the South, "That could not be.
"Slaves are property, bought with our money".
My! My! How could this be!
Such blatant hypocrisy!

We'll find a way to solve this impasse.
The future has to be ensured at any cost.
Property or man—what really is he?
The slave is just what we agree.
And so it was, those leaders so wise
Arrived at the three-fifths compromise.

In 1819 the nation had to face
Another political question involving race.

For statehood Missouri had qualified.
Free state or slave state, they had to decide.
The balance of power Missouri would upset.
A solution would be found—the stage was set.

The House was under Northern control.
The senate was tied; eleven-eleven at the poll.
Cotton production increased by the 'gin'
This fight the Southerners had to win.
The state of Maine did enter free,
Slavery was the lot of Missouri.

The question was settled once and for all
By the terrible conflict—the Civil War.
The war was over, the North had won.
Credit should go to President Lincoln.
In that war many Blacks did fight
To procure for themselves that which was right.

A new day dawned with reconstruction
The future seemed bright for every man.
Ten years of progress the Blacks did enjoy,
As long as the troops the North did deploy.
Ability and ambition the Blacks proved they had.
Reconstruction did make every heart glad.

In 1877 another political question
Destroyed the rights of Afro-Americans.
The troops were withdrawn, southern power restored.
The privileges of Blacks went through the door.
Segregation and discrimination became the rule,
Shattered were dreams of college and school.

Jim Crow became the way of life
For every Afro-American and his wife.
Decades of suffering they did endure
Till they decided they would take it no more.
The new age began with Rosa Parks,
A woman of courage who made her mark.

Remember whenever you read history,
To examine the causes, how things came to be.
Society today is a reflection
Of man's inhumanity to another man.
Go back Afro-Americans if you are wise,
And read all you can about political compromise.

The Fugitive Slave Laws

A new age began in seventeen ninety-three
It was a turning point in Southern history.
Eli Whitney invented the cotton gin,
Soon cotton became the southern king.
For slaves there was a great demand,
Planters were promised great rewards.

Regulations for slaves the planters lacked
So congress passed the Fugitive Act.
All slaves who chose to run away
Could be returned to their masters one fine day.
'Runaways' were no longer legally free
So said the law of seventeen ninety-three.

Many Whites in the North were terribly shocked
At the passage of the New Fugitive Act.
In response, "personal liberty laws", they passed,
Runaways they hoped would be free at last.
Liberty laws the Supreme Court did override.
The federal government supported the planters' side.

Fugitive laws the government again did review.
Stiffer penalties the courts were prepared to issue.
Many Whites had felt such laws were wrong
And helped runaways whenever they ran.
The future for slaves certainly looked dim,
But to terror and injustice they would never give in.

Neither planter, state nor federal law
Could re-impose the bondage which began to thaw
Unjust laws increased the load
On that famous Underground Railroad.
The central point of this story
Is that people will pay any price for liberty.

In Pursuit of Liberty and Happiness

Freedom! Freedom! Oh my! Oh my!
What a place is Illinois!
No master to obey! No homage to pay!
To this state I'll move some happy day.

In Illinois as in Wisconsin,
Men are men, in spite of skin.
Now that I am back in Missouri,
I must face life in slave territory.

Man or property? I know not what!
It is time I find out who is Dread Scott.
For my freedom, tomorrow I'll sue,
Yes! For freedom! My freedom is overdue.

Yes sir! My case I expect to win!
I lived in Illinois and Wisconsin!
If living in 'free states' freedom should bring,
My case in court I am sure to win.

The case was brought before the court supreme.
There I was certain I would achieve my dream.
The case was heard by Chief Justice Taney,
Who had strong views on slavery.

The day came for the court's decision,
'Certainly' I thought 'the case I had won'
"Not so!" Came the answer of the court.
The opposite was the verdict the judges wrote.

Only citizens had the right to sue,
And Scott was not, in the judges' view.
Federal law did not allow Blacks to be
Citizens of this nation—even if born free.

A slave you are, a slave you'll be,
Even though you visited free territory,

Now that you are back in Missouri,
Missouri's law will apply to you.

"Where-ever you are", argued Judge Taney,
"A slave you are and a slave you'll be.
Slave owners have rights to property
Where-ever they are in this country".

Thus declared this judge so "wise",
Unconstitutional—the Missouri Compromise.
A slave is a slave wherever he may be,
In free state or slave state, in this country.

"We hold these truths to be self-evident
That all men are created equal!"
Were those words intended for me?
Am I man or property?

The courts decide questions of liberty!
The truth is here for all to see!
My name is Dread Scott! Who am I really?
Am I man or property?

CHAPTER-11

Sources of Inspiration

The following poems are about the lives of two outstanding African Americans. Both individuals rose from a situation of adversity to become individuals who have left their mark on history.

What they had in common was their dedication to the service of others.

Fredrick Douglas rose from slavery to become a great orator, abolitionist, and finally this nation's ambassador to Haiti.

Harriet Tubman rose from slavery to become a fighter for freedom, a scout and spy during the Civil War, and finally a true example of a person who put service before self.

Frederick Douglass

Before the end of slavery,
A little light began to glow,
It continued to increase in brilliance,
Even under Jim Crow.
It was against the law of slavery,
To teach the Blacks to read;
Everything possible was done,
To kill the academic seed.

Masters feared what would happen
If slaves were given a chance,
And so they all planned it,
To keep Blacks in ignorance.
No matter how hard they tried,
Their efforts were doomed to fail,
Read on my dear reader
And learn of one we hail.

Frederick had a Mistress,
Who really could not see
What harm there was in teaching
Frederick his A B C's.
Frederick's master rebuked her,
For committing such a crime,
"Your efforts will prove dangerous,
If given enough time."

Frederick heard and could not see
What danger there could be,
"If however master thinks it's bad,
 It has to be good for me."
Frederick lost his Mistress' help
So he turned to little white boys,
Who continued to teach him
While they played with their toys.

Lloyd E. Afflick

From his friends he learned enough,
To continue on his own;
Frederick became a great success,
Because the seeds were early sown.
Great orator, and abolitionist,
Great champion of women's rights,
He was a leading figure
In the Emancipation fight.

His efforts and achievements,
Earned him great respect.
To the end he worked for his people,
As you certainly might expect.
His commitment and sincerity,
Were thought of very highly
And so he was made Ambassador,
To the people of Haiti.

Frederick was an example,
Of a slave who rose to the top.
Great talent and ambition
Oppression cannot stop.
When life's problems you encounter,
Think of Frederick Douglass.
He proved, that if you work towards it,
Your goal you'll achieve at last.

Harriet Tubman—A True Hero!!!

Harriet was born in eighteen twenty,
One of eleven—a very large family.
A slave she was born, a slave she refused to be,
She soon risked death to obtain liberty.
Fugitive slave laws she was willing to defy,
The journey to the North she was willing to try.

In 1848 she did join a "load"
On that famous Underground Railroad.
Exciting was the ride on the freedom train
Never! Never would she be a slave again.
Her journey was planned by a White Quaker.
Harriet ended up in Philadelphia.

She gave no thought to personal safety,
She planned the freedom of her family.
To the slave South Harriet did return
After the job of a 'conductor' she did learn.
The safety of her sister she did secure
Freedom to enjoy for evermore.

Many trips to the South this brave lady did make.
Hundreds of slaves to the North, Harriet did take;
Brothers and nieces and parents too,
She brought to the North to start anew.
Friends, strangers and Uncle Dan,
Traveled North with Harriet Tubman.

Word of her success spread throughout the South
Her reputation she earned! There was no doubt.
To Northerners she was the hero of the age!
In the South, she appeared on the 'wanted' page!
The former slave from Maryland,
An exceptional woman! If ever there was one.

Sick soldiers she helped during the Civil War,
There too her performance was that of a star.

She was a spy and a Northern Scout
Much harm she caused the army of the South.
The war was over! The Blacks were free!
The rest of her life she dedicated to humanity.

As a child she could not go to school,
So education for Blacks became her first rule.
She always believed in doing what was right.
She opened a 'home' for Blacks and Whites.
The years passed and Harriet grew old;
The story of her life, many children she told.

She finally died at age 93
Still doing her best to make others happy.
An important lesson her life should be,
Service to others should be our priority!
Harriet! I think the world should know,
That you are truly a national hero.

The Underground Railroad System

Escaping Slaves: Passengers, Freight, Load, Packages

Station: Homes, Churches, Barns, Attics, Cellars—where slaves were hidden

Conductors: People who helped the escaping slaves

Underground Railroad: System of escape organized and operated by people (black and white) who were opposed to slavery.

Lloyd E. Afflick

Reconstruction

The Civil War finally ended; the Union was saved.
The path to the future, President Lincoln had paved.
Thousands of Afro-Americans had paid the ultimate price,
It was freedom or death! There was no other choice.
Radical Republicans early saw their chance,
Along with the Bureau, they worked for Black advance.
Johnson's plan of Reconstruction, they would not tolerate
His plan for Southern pardon, was simply based on hate.

Children of Africa were no longer property.
They were now members of the human family.
Gone were the days of the Confederacy,
The stage was set for true Democracy.
The sorrows of the plantation had ended at last,
Some Blacks had become members of the ruling class.
In the House and Senate some had found a place,
They could now represent the down trodden race.

The 13th Amendment, 'persons' of slaves made,
Amendment 14, citizen rights to Blacks gave.
The 15th Amendment conferred voting rights,
Future decision to be made by registered Blacks and Whites.
Four thousand schools in the South the Bureau began,
The right to an education the Blacks had won.
Three thousand teachers to the South early did go,
A part of the work of the Freedmen's Bureau.

Great was the sacrifice the Blacks did make,
Their future on education they were willing to stake.
A period of hope if ever there was one,
Thus was the period of Reconstruction.
Proud were the Blacks of their legislators
One did achieve the position of Lieutenant Governor.
Oh what a joy it was to be alive and free!
The future looked bright; as bright as could be.

And just as fate had planned it! It was not meant to last,
America soon returned to its dreadful past.
The post-war experiment in justice and fair play,
Seemed to have died slowly, with every passing day.
The North's concern was now its investment capital,
No longer the champion of the Afro American.
America's soul had been put to the acid test,
It failed miserably to live up to its best.

Stillborn was "true" American Democracy,
Missed was an opportunity for racial harmony.
The election of '76 decided the South's fate,
Creating a vicious system based on hate.
Politics triumphed over principle,
Showing the world America's true mettle.
Today we are haunted by those leaders wise
Those leaders who made The 77 Compromise*.

*The Compromise

The Compromise refers to the 1877 Compromise. It was agreed under the 1877 Compromise by leaders of both political parties that the Federal forces would be withdrawn from the South, and the former Confederate leaders would be restored to positions of power. This set the stage for the Jim Crow Era to begin.

The Jim Crow South

This is a story about which you should know,
It is the story of Southern Jim Crow.
Southern leaders developed a political plan,
A plan to destroy the Afro Americans.
They tried to destroy Black political strength,
So they undermined the 15th Amendment.

First, there was the ridiculous "Grandfather Clause".
This was simply discriminatory State laws.
Then there were mandatory literacy tests,
Difficult to pass even by the Southern best.
The poll tax was there to further ensure
Black Americans would be able to vote no more.

Thus it was that one by one
Southern states did over-ride the Constitution.
The plan was simple; Throughout the South
 Suppress the Black vote, encourage the white 'turn out'
And just in case laws were not enough,
Hate groups were relied on, to do "their stuff.

Wherever one went there were always signs,
A constant reminder not to cross the color line.
And so it was for over 75 years,
Afro-Americans did shed a whole lot of tears.
Black success during Reconstruction
For-ever and ever was sadly gone.

Sad it was that in their plight
The Supreme Court failed to support Black rights.
And so it was that a system was born
A system in which Blacks were regarded with scorn.
One's life chances were now limited by race,
Your badge forever, was the color of your face.

The situation at the middle of the 20th century
Was the direct result of official policy.

Southern leaders never would agree
That Blacks also had the right to be free.
Semi-slaves forever Blacks should be,
The corner stone of Southern economy.

Looking back over American History
Great errors are there for all to see.
Today, race would not be such a problem,
If a century ago it was not "we" against "them".
Reconstruction opened wide opportunity's door
It was closed in 77* unfortunately, to be sure.

*77 refers to the 1877 Compromise.

Lloyd E. Afflick

We Are One!!

We are one! Oh children of Africa—
Scattered throughout the Diaspora.
Separated we are by land and sea,
The tragic result of history.
Focused we are on nationality,
Contrary to the thoughts of Marcus Garvey.
These were his words to you and to me,
"One God! One aim! One destiny!"

Though for centuries we have been apart,
We're always together, one at heart.
For a very long time attempts were made,
To reach out to one another as Garvey said.
In seventeen seventy two, Lord Mansfield's decree,
Freed Blacks in England automatically.
Freedom for Blacks created a problem,
The British knew not what to do with them.

Free they were but without a home,
And so they were sent to Sierra Leone.
This was the sneaky beginning
Of early British colonialism.
They planted the seeds of British culture
In the heart of West Africa.
Glad they were to be home at last,
Africa to be influence by their past.

Reports were heard wherever one went,
About the success of the experiment.
The idea caught on in America,
As a result came Liberia.
"Free Blacks" in America were not really free
They lived a life of total misery.
Hundreds of Blacks to Liberia were sent
To solve America's problem of embarrassment.

Settlers came from far and near
Liberia's freedom they wished to share.
Liberia became an important place
To people world-wide of the African race.
Richard Blyden, Joseph Campbell, and Martin Delaney
Were important leaders of the Nineteenth Century.
The ideas they shared with everyone
Were early concepts of Pan African.

Jamaica's Garvey was a black nationalist.
Dr. DuBois, Educator and Pan Africanist,
Carter Woodson, Father of Black History,
Claude McKay, prolific writer of poetry,
George Padmore, Peter Millard, and T.R. Makonnen
Got students together, organizations to begin.
They all believed in 'togetherness',
They tried to instill African consciousness.

Senghor, Nkrumah, Azikiwe and many of the best
Were influenced by ideas of brothers from the west.
The love of Africa and of liberty
Was not destroyed by centuries of slavery.
Let's bring an end to parochialism,
Created by European colonialism.
My brothers and sisters wherever you may be
Remember the words of Marcus Mosiah Garvey,
"One God! One aim! One Destiny!"

Different Approaches to a Common Goal

The following two poems are about the lives and contributions of Booker T. Washington and Dr. W.E.B. DuBois.

As was the case with Dr. Martin Luther King Jr. and Malcolm X, Booker T Washington and Dr. W.E.B. DuBois both were aiming at the same goal. They were the products of different times and different circumstances. Quite naturally, their approaches to the improvement of the life chances of their people differed greatly.

However, both were committed to the removal of the inequalities, deprivation, and oppression to which African Americans were subjected.

Booker T. Washington

Booker T.?
What manner of man was he really?
Was he, as Dr. Du Bois said,
A leader who, his people he misled
Caring more about the interests of the Whites
Neglecting totally his people's Civil Rights?

If early childhood, you do agree
Influences greatly one's personality,
Then it should not be hard to see
The circumstances which created Booker T.
Should we judge him by what he said?
Or by his positive deeds instead?

Booker taught himself to read,
Believing that would help him succeed.
Educated at the Hampton Institute,
There he learnt, what to him was "society's truths"
As founder and Principal of Tuskegee
He adopted Hampton's philosophy.

"Practical education was the key
To future Black prosperity.
Do the best at whatever you can,
Nothing beats working with the hand.
Avoid the fight for social equality,
Be careful in choosing your priority"

"To segregation I will turn a blind eye,
If for survival on 'you' I can rely."
Booker grew in power and fame
While he played the political game.
He was disliked by the extreme Left and Right.
By radical Blacks and reactionary Whites

Black opposition began to grow,
With the rising tide of Jim Crow.

Booker was the hero of white society,
They liked his idea of 'postponing' equality,
Booker certainly was an astute politician,
Secretly he wanted to change the laws of the land.

In spite of his image, where-ever he went
He worked for the goals of the Talented Tenth
What some saw as a lack of ideal
To the Whites was his greatest appeal.
Of Southern power Booker was always aware,
In attempting change, he took great care.

Often Booker was severely criticized,
Yet his gradual approach might have been wise
What would be the result of open confrontation,
When the South had power to defy the Constitution?
How could Blacks fight the powers of Jim Crow?
It was better to live, dreaming of tomorrow.

Courageous men were Du Bois and Trotter,
Foremost leaders of Niagara.
Both were academics and idealists;
On the other hand Booker was a realist.
Du Bois and Trotter were of the 20th century
Booker was the product of Southern slavery.

While to the world he showed one face
Behind the scene he worked for his race.
Like Trotter and Du Bois he believed in Civil Rights
He was however, aware of the power of the Whites.
He too was intent on changing the laws,
So he contested the Grandfather Clause.

To work with the hands' was no disgrace,
This idea he instilled in people of his race.
His personal funds he often did use,
To bring to an end racial abuse.
He gave dignity and purpose to life
In a society beset by racial strife.

Booker earned for himself great respect,
Even from those you would least expect.
'Up From Slavery', his autobiography
Greatly influenced Marcus Mosiah Garvey.
Garvey's visit was to meet this great man.
Sad to say Booker had just passed on.

A man of power and great intrigue
He greatly influenced The National Negro Business League.
Yet to this man there was another side,
The good he did, he preferred to hide.
For the good of his people, his money he spent
Of this little was known! He kept it silent.

Booker T. lived through the last years of slavery.
He lived to become a leader in the early 20th century.
He experienced Reconstruction, Jim Crow and World War 1
Think of him then as the Transitional man.
As a leader he was greatly misunderstood.
Although for his people, he did the best that he could.

Booker T. was a natural born strategist,
His actions were based on careful analysis.
He understood the political realities of his day,
And saw co-operation, not conflict, as the only way
You may admire him! With his ideals you may disagree!
Whatever you think; he too worked for Black equality.

Dr. "William E. B. DuBois
Freedom and Justice for All

In 1868 a baby boy was born,
Destined to be the first "Light of dawn".
As a scholar he was among America's best,
He would later be known in the East and West.
At Harvard, Fisk, and the University of Berlin,
Academic distinctions he often would win.
Versatile scholar he proved to be,
An authority on Afro American History.

A brilliant teacher and writer was he,
At the famous Atlanta University.
There he influenced many young minds,
Producing scholars of his own kind.
In knowledge and wisdom he did mellow,
Becoming later a National Fellow.
His years of teaching helped him prepare,
For a future demanding political career.

With Booker T's views he vehemently disagreed,
A campaign for equality he was about to lead.
Black America would no longer accept Jim Crow,
Discrimination and segregation had to go.
'Day after day we will continue to fight
Until Afro Americans receive their constitutional rights.
Afro Americans also have brilliant minds,
We refuse to be treated like an inferior kind.'

In 1905 a decisive step was made,
Preparations for the future were very well laid.
A conference was planned for Niagara.
It was a meeting of the Black Intelligentsia.
W.M. Trotter and W.B. DuBois,
Their intellect and courage they were about to deploy.
A message to Jim Crow was about be sent,
By these representatives of the **Talented Tenth.**

For our constitutional rights we now make claim,
White rights and Black rights **Must** be the same.
Separation of Americans now must cease,
If in this land there should be justice and peace.
The battle lines with Jim Crow now were drawn,
The days of submission were certainly gone.
In a new direction Afro Americans were led,
No longer Booker T; it was DuBois instead.

The political demands expressed at Niagara,
Were soon to be heard from Florida to California.
In 1909 came the NAACP
Its spiritual leader was DuBois WEB.
As Director of Research and Publicity,
He championed the cause of Black liberty.
Dr. DuBois' was a very great mind,
Spent entirely in the service of mankind.

Colonialism in Africa was a major concern,
And so to such problems his attention he did turn.
From leader of the struggle of the Afro American,
To champion of the Movement, Pan African.
Contented as a leader he could not be
Until colonial Africa was finally free.
This was a man by all standards great,
He left this world in a far better state.

CHAPTER-12

Grandpa and Jimmy talk about the African American experience.

Dr. Carter G. Woodson
A Source of Inspiration

It is 1945. The Second World War has just ended. Jimmy's Granddad is reading his newspaper, with the youngster looking on. Granddad smiles.

Jimmy:
What is so funny in that newspaper Grandpa?

Granddad:
Jimmy my boy, the war is over. Our boys' performance was better than anyone imagined Jimmy. Even the biased press had to acknowledge their spectacular achievement.

Jimmy:
What are you talking about Grandpa?

Granddad:
This article! (Granddad reads the headline) "The Negro Squadron Performed With Distinction."

Jimmy:
So what is funny about that Grandpa?

Granddad:
Jimmy, my boy, I smile because I am happy. Before the war, Negro soldiers were criticized for not having the intelligence to fight even as infantrymen. Now they have distinguished themselves as the best in the Air Force.

Jimmy:
Granddad, Please tell me more. (Granddad tells the story of the Tuskegee Airmen)

Granddad:
Jimmy, you are too young to understand. The journey of our people to this point has been a terrible one. It began 300 years ago when the first Africans were enslaved in this land.

Jimmy, my boy, I need not go back that far. You will get an idea of what I'm talking about, if I tell you Dr. Woodson's life story.

Jimmy:

Please Grandpa, let me hear Dr. Woodson's story. I have always wondered how he made it to that great University at a time when most of our people could not get a chance even to learn their ABC's.

Granddad:

I am glad to know you have been thinking about the past. It is only by so doing that you will appreciate how far we have come, and be able to resolve to do even better than I have done.

Jimmy:

I am glad that I asked, why you were smiling. Now I am about to hear something I have always wondered about!

Granddad:

Please ask me any question about the story as I go along.

Jimmy:

Yes sir, **I** will.

Granddad:

Dr. Woodson was born 136 years ago, the son of two newly freed slaves. Life for ex-slaves was tough. They had no lands, no education, no money, and there were very few people who really cared about them.

*Granddad tells Dr. Woodson's life story using the style of the **Griots of traditional Africa.***

Tell Me Grandpa

Grandpa! Grandpa! Ah . . . . Let me see?
Let's talk about Afro American History!
"Oh my child I'll be happy to please.
Educating you brings pleasure to me."

Tell me Sir, tell me about Black equality;
What it really was like at the turn of the century?
Did America's growing industrial might
Bridge the gap between Blacks and Whites?

My boy, your question makes me laugh,
Your thoughts are so very, very far off.
Blacks continued to be citizen second-class,
Their future a reflection of their horrible past.
The Courts decision of eighteen ninety six
Their inferior position legally fixed.
To northern cities thousands did migrate
In a desperate attempt to escape racial hate.

Thousands served in the First World War,
They gained experience in countries afar.
Their experience prepared them later to face
Domestic problems based on race.
African American veterans were soon to realize
That their service changed nothing, in Jim Crow's eyes.
In the South life became a living hell.
Read the life and times of Ida B. Wells.

The Urban League, the NAACP
And individuals such as Marcus Garvey,
Segregation and discrimination would no longer accept—
Equal rights for Blacks they would now fight to get.
And thus it was that the struggle began,
A struggle to ensure justice for all Americans.
America's government now had to face
The consequences of its polices based on race.

My dear Grandpa I still cannot see,
What brought the change in official policy.
For fifty years as we all do know
The Supreme Court did allow Jim Crow.

Good question you ask my dear grandson.
 I'll answer your question the best way I can.
The Great Depression of 1929
Started a spiral of economic decline.
Hunger and suffering swept the land,
It's hard for you really to understand.
President Roosevelt offered the nation a New Deal
His plan to the Blacks had special appeal.

Gradually the economy began to rebound
The secret to recovery the President had found.
Yet second-class citizens Blacks continued to be
In-spite of the Constitution's well known decree.
A march on Washington was soon planned,
The aim was to force the President's hand.
Roosevelt, his preference now had to show,
It was justice for all or racist Jim Crow!

President Roosevelt provided for the first time
An opportunity for Blacks to speak their mind.
A. Philip Randolph of the Black Union Exec.
With the New Deal President finally met.
The plight of the Blacks was brought to light
The government had its chance to do what was right.
And so it was that the President did agree
To form The Fair Employment Practices Committee.

It was Roosevelt who took the first timid step;
We wondered then, if his promises would be kept.
As Afro Americans we could not look back,
We had suffered enough because we were Black.
Segregation and discrimination continued apace
While in Government Black leaders were placed.
Bethune, Hastie, Weaver and Horne,
Represented our interests in Washington.

To Tell you the truth my dear Grandpa
Roosevelt did little to end Jim Crow.
Since Southern leaders would never freely give in
How did the fight for Civil Rights begin?

The fight for freedom really began
With the enslavement of the first proud African.
Bondage and oppression our people tried to resist
But they could not fight guns with their shackled wrists.
And so throughout the plantation days
Control was maintained in various ways.
Segregation and discrimination under Jim Crow
Could not deter us from the freedom we once knew.

Remember my child the fight once begun
Was to continue until victory was won.
President Truman faced the problem squarely.
He outlawed discrimination in the US Army.
Legal changes there had to be,
That was the role of NAACP.
Battles were fought to change the laws
The first to go was the Grandfather Clause.

For fifty long years the struggle went on,
Cases were lost and cases were won.
And then a landmark case was won;
The famous Brown vs. Board of Education.
For nearly sixty years the Pleasy Case
Provided segregation with a legal base.
And then came the year 1954,
"Separate but Equal"—was law no more.

Hail to you Justice Thurgood Marshall!
Your name shall be remembered after you're gone.
Noble son of our people that you are
In the struggle for justice you have played your part.
Problems there are and problems there will be
The struggle will continue till we all are free.
"America! America! Land of Equality?"
If such is the case convince my grandson, my little Jimmy.

Carter G. Woodson

Woodson Carter G?
What kind of a child was he?
Come on Grandpa, I promise to be good.
Share his story! If you want, I know you could.
Jimmy my boy, how could I say "no"
To a question like that, that will help you grow?

"Sit down my boy and listen to me,
While I tell you Carter's story.
The children of Africa were finally free,
After two centuries as human property.
Of jobs and homes there was no guarantee,
All they had were their church, their music and families."

Into such a situation Carter was born,
The evils of slavery were not really gone.
At work he spent his childhood years,
No time to enjoy childhood affairs.
Yet while he toiled through those difficult years,
Of the future he had no reason to fear.

Carter taught himself to write and read,
Believing that to SUCCESS these skills would lead.
At age twenty he entered Douglass High,
On ambition he hoped to soar to the sky.
Education he soon began to see,
As the pathway to true liberty.

Time to waste there really was none,
It was work, no school, no teenage fun.
Mine worker, school teacher, Principal of Douglass High,
His thirst for knowledge he had begun to satisfy.
So off he went to Chicago U,
There to develop his point of view.

His mission in life he began to see,
Was the study of Afro-American History.

Only by acquiring knowledge of the past,
Our ancestor's culture he would firmly grasp.
The future of Africa's children in America,
Rests on their knowledge of African culture.

Travel and experience are other ways,
To prepare the mind for future days.
"To the Philippines, Africa and France I will go,
To broaden my horizon; my intellect to grow."
Years of experience in those foreign lands,
Helped him to see the plight of Afro-Americans.

Carter returned to the U.S. of A.,
To prepare himself for the part he'd play.
"The answers to questions about society,
Are all to be found by studying history."
Great ambition, persistence and tenacity,
Were soon to be rewarded with a P.H.D.

Success Carter knew was a condition of the mind,
Think as a scholar, even while working in the mine.
"Children of Africa must begin to see,
The tragic effects of centuries of slavery.
Perpetual suffering is not your fate,
It's only maintained by ignorance and hate."

"If this nation's wounds must begin to heal,
It will only be done if its problems are revealed.
Perhaps it's my purpose; my destiny,
James and Eliza's son; Woodson Carter G.
I'll fight this fight; the struggle must begin!
My chief weapons; just paper and pen"

Ridicule, opposition, rejection and more,
Only strengthened his resolve - success to ensure.
His quality of life was of the simplest,
His clothes, his food and his place of rest.
Life's usual pleasures had to take second place,
To the future up-liftment of the African race.

Books, journals and papers he wrote,
The importance of Africa he hoped to promote.
Associations, organizations he did begin
The minds of America, he hoped to win.
Children of Africa be no longer blind,
Reclaim your place in the story of mankind.

Doctors and lawyers and humble farm hands,
Must learn the truth across this land.
Through classrooms, pulpits, and word of mouth,
The story will be told; there is no doubt.
Blacks and whites must be made to see,
The oneness of all humanity.

And so it was that Carter G.,
Came face to face with his destiny.
Segregation and discrimination could not stop,
This visionary from arriving at the top.
"My people's dignity I am here to reclaim,
It is time to end this political game."

Recapture your past taught Carter G.,
Africans were great throughout history.
Her influence was felt from Greece to Rome;
Wake up; be proud of your fore-father's home.
Pride and courage will be restored,
When Africa's story is correctly told.

His crowning glory finally began,
It was a special celebration for Afro-Americans.
Hail to you Dr. Carter G.,
Educator, author, Father of Black History.
Poverty and oppression could not stop,
A disciplined dreamer from reaching the top.

Farm hand and miner till age twenty,
Finally to Harvard for his P.H.D.
Dear reader, it should be plain for you to see,
You eventually become what you <u>choose</u> to be.
So believe it and you will achieve it,
In this land of opportunity.

Believe it and you will achieve it,
In this the twenty first century.

The African Americans

The poem, The African Americans, traces the journey of people of African heritage in the United States of America from the birth of the nation to the Civil Rights Movement (1776-1955).

Using highlights of the contributions of some outstanding African Americans as its theme, the poem shows that not even the dehumanization of slavery can stop an individual from succeeding if there is the will, and the opportunity presents itself.

The lesson to you reader is—if slavery, segregation, discrimination, and planned deprivation of educational opportunities could not stop those individuals from succeeding, nothing should be able to stop you, now (21st century) that most of the barriers have been removed.

The Afro-Americans

Let me tell you a story as it has never been told,
It is a story worth hearing by the young and the old.
Think about it as often as you can,
It is the story of the Afro-American.

From many places they were brought and sold,
Made to labor for others from youth till they grew old.
Against England's tyranny the colonists did resist
The first to die was Attucks—dear noble Chris.

In seventeen-seventy five hostilities began,
Eight years later victory was won.
At Lexington, Concord, and Bunker hill too
The Blacks were willing to pay "freedom's due".

Life for ex-slaves in America was tough,
"To Africa they should go" thought Paul Cuffe.
Ship's captain and owner, such a man was he,
He cared for others and so should we.

Bought and enslaved was Phillis Wheatly,
World famous poetess she grew up to be.
A great man of science was Banneker, Mr. B.,
Education he saw as the way to victory.

To court went Dred Scott to prove he was free,
Back came the answer, the court did not agree.
Sojourner Truth as her name suggests,
Spoke the truth wherever she found rest.

A very brilliant man was Frederick Douglass,
From slave to leader he rose in a flash.
In courage and oratory he surely did excel,
His people from slavery he fought to expel.

'Technical education' insisted Booker T.,
"Will solve all problems, in this land of misery."

A very great scholar was Dr. DuBois,
"Full rights for all", was his daily call.

"Recapture your past", taught Woodson Carter G.,
A brilliant historian and teacher was he.
Each year you celebrate Afro-American History,
Remember Carter Woodson, he gave it to you.

A man of the Arts was Paul Dumbar,
James Weldon Johnson certainly went far.
Langston Hughes was Harlem's literary best,
In music Duke Ellington led all the rest.

Mary Bethune was a born educator,
Boys and girls I wish you'd emulate her.
She was admired by all wherever she went,
Soon she became friend of the President.

"To the back of the bus no longer I'll go",
So said Rosa, and sat by the door.
This act of courage really did start,
A man named Martin on a very new path.

Martin Luther King Jr. What a man was he!
He gave his life to help you be what you want to be.
He used the strategies of Mahatma Gandhi,
To secure freedom for you and freedom for me.

Malcolm X was the Shining Black Prince,
Before the power struggle he never would wince.
"Love yourself and get an education",
And as Garvey said "Up you mighty nation".

Thousands more have contributed to the past,
Records of their service forever are lost.
They all sacrificed that forever you'll be,
In this land of promise—forever free.

Dr. Martin Luther King, Jr. The Soul of America

A man of courage, wisdom and great faith,
With unconditional love he embraced those who hate.
Freedom and justice for everyone,
Was his goal for all in this fair land.
'Red and Yellow, White and Black,
Their value should be measured by the way they act.

Intellectual power, early he began to show,
His thinking was influenced by Gandhi and Henry Thoreau.
Born at a time when the races were apart,
Correcting this evil was the goal he sought.
Himself for service he did prepare,
Fate seemed to have planned his leadership career.

It was nearly a century since the Civil War,
Yet from the evils of slavery Afro-Americans did not get far.
Segregation, discrimination and untold despair,
Were burdens of life seen almost everywhere.
Dark clouds overshadowed the Plantation South,
Suddenly there was a dramatic turnabout.

And just as if by a stroke of fate,
The system began to crumble; it was based on hate.
Montgomery was where it all began,
A struggle for the freedom of African-Americans.
They prayed! They marched! They also did sing,
The struggle was led by Dr. Martin Luther King.

"Give love for hate—the buses boycott!!
Use spiritual power; it's the only weapon we have got.
There is strength in unity; let's continue to fight,
Victory will be ours because we are right."
Twelve long months after the struggle began,
The Supreme Court's verdict—African Americans had won.

Intellectual, orator, spiritual leader was he,
Along with his people, he applied Gandhi's philosophy.
'Freedom and justice we will achieve one day,
If we continue to fight the non-violent way."
'We Shall Over Come' they all did sing,
This was the message of Dr. Martin Luther King.

From Montgomery to Birmingham the movement he led,
To end segregation and build integration instead.
Clubs and dogs, water hoses and guns!!
Instruments of violence, the marchers had none.
The brutal attacks daily the nation did see,
The power of non-violence was shown on T.V.

As leader of the movement—the S.C.L.C,
He continued to rely on the non-violent philosophy.
Supporters of oppression soon admitted they were wrong,
They were soon defeated by prayer and song.
On the youth of the nation now the movement would rely,
It was freedom and justice or they were willing to die.

The challenge in Selma was a very special case,
It was confrontation of a system based on race.
Lack of protection, intimidation and daily threats,
Could not deter them—they preferred to accept death.
In a new direction the nation was ready to go,
This was impossible as long as there was Jim Crow.

August 28th of the year nineteen sixty three,
Will forever be remembered in American history.
Red and Yellow, Black and White,
On Washington descended, demanding Civil Rights.
Believers in justice—quarter million strong,
Lifted their voices in prayer and song.

And so at the end of that special day,
A very special voice loudly was heard to say
"From the hills and valleys let freedom ring"
It was the voice of Dr. Martin Luther King.
His passion, his faith, his love did galvanize,
A spiritual connection nationwide.

Leaders of the nation responded at last,
They responded to the cries of the oppressed class.
For justice and fair play Dr. Martin continued to call,
"It's time to break down the segregation wall".

And so it was that new laws were passed—
Laws to end America's dreadful past.

Civil Rights and Voting Rights did clear the way
For the sun to rise on a brand new day.
Victory after victory non-violence had won,
It was now time for a broader liberation plan.
Support for the poor of Memphis Tennessee—
Was the next plan of action of this visionary.

Passive resistance had served its day,
Black Power!! Black Panther!!—presented another way.
Matters of the poor and the war overseas
Soon had become the new priorities.
His role on the stage this great man had played,
The path to the future he had successfully laid.

His earthly mission accomplished—he seemed to see,
He told it to the people of Memphis Tennessee.
"I have been to the mountain top; I have seen the Promised Land,
"I may not get there with you—but I want you to know,
That WE as a people will get to the Promised Land."
His message to us—"For whatever is right, take a stand.'

His mission accomplished, this great man passed on,
Leaving behind his people to carry on.
He played his part, now he is gone,
He set an example for us and the yet unborn.
Injustice and despair are the parents of HOPE
Knowledge of your history will help you to cope.

Yes!! Believe it!!
Knowledge of your history will help you to cope.

CHAPTER-13

Contemporary U S A

The USA today is home to people from every corner of the earth, (representing most cultures and speaking most of the world's languages). With the exception of the Native Americans who it is estimated arrived over 20,000 years ago, all the nation's people arrived within the last 500 years.

In spite of the growing pains this nation experienced, and in some cases continues to experience—(slavery, Civil War, segregation, discrimination, racism)—the movement towards acceptance of all people has been quite encouraging. As is the case in all societies, there are periodic conflicts between individuals and between groups.

At the national level however, there seems to be a 'oneness' of purpose. Perhaps it is this common goodwill of the individual for the welfare of the group (nation) which gives meaning to the name United States of America. Racial linguistic, religious differences, differences in cultural heritage all take second place to American nationality.

Perhaps the success of this nation (the USA) is the direct result of the principles enshrined in the nation's Constitution. Law rather than tradition is the principle upon which the society operates. All individuals are therefore free to pursue their own happiness as long as they do it within the context of the law.

The above is not to suggest that life in the USA is perfect. No matter what the law says, no matter how law abiding the citizens are; allowance must be made for the failings or unreasonable behavior of individuals or groups. So, though the nation remains united and strong, there are constant occurrences of human failings. The following poems:
She Was American Too
John Public's Response to the Evening News
Dad's Wheelchair
Someone's Son
Were all inspired by human failings which were considered important enough <u>to make the evening news</u>.

She Was an American Too

She lived there for many years,
Yet no one really seemed to care.
For over four years she was dead—
No one for her, the last rites read.
Her brothers reported seeing her last,
Fourteen years before, when their mother 'passed'.

Trash in her house piled up high,
No one cared to find the reason why.
Her mail she never did collect,
Neither her Social Security checks.
Many thought she had gone to live,
Where in life, to her a job did give.

"She preferred to be left alone",
So for seven years her neighbor never did phone.
Someone turned her water off.
From the house came not even a cough.
The bank began to have serious doubts,
When she never checked on her bank account.

When to her house they finally did go,
She had died. How? No one really knows.
There, before them was a pile of bones,
The remains of a woman who had lived alone.
No final rites; no one to mourn,
No grave marked with the usual headstone.

This silent death is a sad commentary
On the state of this our society.
Sad it is that our major concern
Is the money that we daily earn.
It is time that we begin to care,
And our lives with neighbors willingly share.

What is the purpose of our birth?
Why are we really upon this earth?
Is it daily wealth to accumulate
And leave the world in the same state?
All great people in history,
Were concerned about more than—**"me'**

John Public's Response to the Evening News

Boy shot Police just for fun!

Where on earth did he get the gun?
Hope the Judge will have no mercy!
Lock him up and throw away the key!

Teenager rapes woman 85 years old!

How could his heart be so cold?
Show the beast no sympathy!
Lock him up and throw away the key!

Gang member shoots at teacher in school!

He has got to be some kind of a fool.
Hope the Judge will have no mercy!
Lock him up and throw away the key!

Girl charged for shooting tourist!

Oh my God! What kind of a place is this?
Show the beast no sympathy!
Lock her up and throw away the key!

Youth terrorized affluent neighborhood!

I would kill that sucker if I could.
Hope the Judge will have no mercy!
Lock him up and throw away the key!

Boy kills friend at birthday party!

What unbridled youthful jealousy!
Show the beast no sympathy!
Lock him up and throw away the key!

Boy 10 smashed windshield with a brick!

All he needs is a real good kick!
Hope the Judge will show no mercy!
Lock him up and throw away the key!

Boy killed baby because it cried!

I bet he'll say—'The Police lied'?
Show the beast no sympathy!
Lock him up and throw away the key!

Boy 14, stole over a dozen cars.

Among his peers he is a star.
Hope the Judge will have no mercy!
Lock him up and throw away the key!

Lock him up and throw away the key!!!
That's the immediate response from you and me.
That's not the answer to the problems of society!
The answer is, Improved Communities.

Until from depravity we all are free,
Forget that confounded—key!
No longer will there be a need to fear,
If about others we begin to care.

Dad's Wheelchair

Hard working Dad and his little Sheer,
They certainly were a perfect pair.
Sheer followed him everywhere.
Wherever he went, she was there.

He worked hard to pay for her care,
Of his secure future he had no fear.
He could depend on his daughter Sheer,
Through thick and thin she would be there.

Baseball games; they were always there,
They both loved the open air.
At the stadium, no smokes, no beer,
Not while he was with his little Sheer.

His greatest joy was to hear her cheer,
She amused all who were sitting near.
To that stadium they would always wear
Their most expensive baseball gear.

As the years passed she grew more fair,
Daddy grew prouder of his daughter Sheer.
Still to the stadium year by year—
They both would go and Sheer would cheer.

The shouts of the crowds they loved to hear
Even when Daddy's team people sometimes jeered.
Sheer was always awed by the thousands of chairs,
Chairs were here, there and everywhere.

And so with each passing year,
Dad experienced wear and tear.
Now it was Sheer's time to be sincere
To her Dad who loved her so dear.

There was a shift in the roles of this pair
It was Sheer's time now, her dad to care.
 Caring for her sick Daddy dear—
A job Sheer really did terribly fear.

"Please come here my little Sheer,
Get me my favorite baseball gear.
Come comb your Daddy's thin gray hair.
Daddy wants to go to a special somewhere."

"Come here my fair little Sheer,
You are my only heir.
The shouts of the crowd let's once more hear,
To the game let's go, my daughter dear."

Sheer placed Dad in his old wheelchair
To be pushed to the park was a pleasure rare.
The game was good but Sheer did not cheer.
She sat by her Dad engulfed in fear.

"Excuse me Dad, I will be near".
Dad sat alone, he did not fear.
In a lonesome corner sat Dad's little Sheer
Thoroughly washed in her own tears.

It was not that she did not care,
Her responsibility was too much for her to bear.
She heard the cheers, she heard the jeers.
The game ended; it was calm, everywhere.

She looked at the thousands of stadium chairs,
Like an empty cupboard they all were bare.
She looked at her Daddy sitting there—
Sitting there in that wheelchair.

And then with her eyes full of tears,
She looked at Dad in his wheelchair.
And with her heart full of fear
Daddy's baby left him sitting there.

Sheer left Dad there, in his wheelchair
Left him there in his wheelchair.
Dad there, in his wheelchair.
Sheer left Dad there in his wheelchair.

Sheer left him there, in his wheelchair!!!

Someone's Son

He was born on a drug-infested street,
At his house, hardly was there anything to eat.
Community influence in his formative years,
Set the stage for a future full of tears.

His heroes never, never would he meet,
They were not the type to visit his street.
He was a very intelligent lad,
Influenced less by good than by bad.

His mother he dearly loved,
The best in life he wished she could have.
He became a drug-pushers tool,
Often disobeying the rules of his school.

Soon his talents exploded with a bang!
He regretfully joined the neighborhood gang.
New heroes he began to find,
They were all of the underworld kind.

Another youth, the wrong choice made,
Later he was found in the gutter—dead.
If only someone about him did care,
That mother's child would still be here.

CHAPTER-14

Moving In a New Direction

Everybody can contribute to the building of a better world by doing whatever he/ she can, to build a better self, community, country. All that it takes is the <u>belief</u> that it is possible, and the willingness <u>to work</u> to bring about change.

The following poems are dedicated to:
1) Concerned Citizens
   —Mr. Concern
   —Let's Make a New Start

2) All Teachers
   —An Open Letter to My Teacher

3) Grandparents and Teenagers
   —Please Tell Me Why

4) All Students
   —I Am A Very Special Person

5) Humanity
   —Beautiful, Beautiful, Butterfly

They all suggest ways by which we as citizens together can make this world a better place by serving others or by working to make ourselves better persons.

<u>A Reason to Smile</u> is a reflection on the journey of African Americans over the past 400 years. It summarizes the experiences of African Americans, from their sacrifices and sufferings to their survival and ultimate success in this nation

Mr. Concern

An unusual man was Constantine Stern,
Little children called him Mr. Concern.
He did not attend college or university,
Yet he greatly influenced his community.

He lived a very simple life,
Always there for his children and wife.
He is not remembered for his handsome looks,
What everyone remembers, is his love for books.

Young and old turned to him for advice,
Even those renowned for terrible vice.
A lasting impression he left on all he did meet,
He was respected by all, on his neighborhood street.

Mr. Concern lived by a simple philosophy.
"Do unto others as you would have done to thee.
Put people at the top of your—Priority List,
The quest for things, try hard to resist."

"More from this life is yours to have,
When all people you learn to love."
Mr. Concern died with a smile on his face,
He left this world, a far better place.

Let's Make A New Start

They lived in an affluent neighborhood,
Enjoying all that they possibly could.
Well-furnished homes and beautiful cars—
The type of life of Hollywood Stars.

Yet each day to work they all would go,
To their neighbors, no 'Good Morning' or a simple 'Hello'
John minded his business, and Tom minded his,
Mary tried always to out-dress Liz.

For each other they showed no care,
One another's problems they did not share.
Theirs was a life of affluency,
Yet there really was no true community.

Then it happened! No one thought it would!
Violence struck that neighborhood!
Everyone was duly alarmed—Oh no! Not Here!
Soon they all began to care; caring only out of fear.

At one house they all did meet,
It was the first time on that street.
Out of evil came forth good,
They began to live, as people should.

Dedicated To Foreign Born Students

The poem which follows addresses the feelings, experiences and concerns of foreign born students in schools in the United States of America.

It is dedicated to the students whose first language is other than English as well as some English speaking students whose cultural and educational backgrounds are different from that of the United States of America.

It deals with problems of adjustment and the critical role caring teachers play in helping to guide these students to success.

An Open Letter To my Teacher

Oh! Dear teacher I need your listening ear,
I have tried my best to find someone who really cares:
I speak for Pam, I speak for Juan,
I speak for Maria and I speak for Sam.

Thousands more feel the very same way,
But cannot find words, their feelings to say.
Give us a chance and our part we will play,
Credit to this school we will be some day.

All my life I was called Melissa Grant,
Here, I'm called—child of an immigrant.
All my life of my language I was proud
Here, I am afraid to speak aloud.

In your class I try my best
To get good grades on every test.
I don't do well—although I try,
For what reason, I cannot say why.

Perhaps it is because of the pressures I feel,
Reasons for which I am unable to reveal.
In this school it is hard to remember,
Perhaps because I am just another number.

In my land I used to do well,
I come here and no one could tell.
The things I learned matter no more,
Everyone thinks I am stupid, I am sure.

Geography and History were favorites of mine,
Today in these subjects I have certainly declined.
Of my land and people no more I hear,
Oh! Dear teacher—I think that's unfair.

To school each day I will certainly come,
But believe it, to me school is no fun.

Lloyd E. Afflick

We children from abroad have much to share
We come with knowledge from nearly everywhere.

Frustration on faces each day I see
Believe me teacher the cause is not of you.
A reservoir of knowledge is here yet untapped.
Yet many of us feel, forever trapped.

Sharing with others will make us feel,
Important as others: Teacher is that a deal?
When all in this class feel important,
Our confidence will grow, the way you want.

Teacher, on you I hope I can depend,
If not, my dreams for the future will certainly end.
A reply to my letter I may never get,
On your concern for my future I hope I can bet.

Please Tell Me Why

I think of life and I wonder why,
What reason is there daily to try.
Why endure the stress I face,
Merely to win the education race?
Why an academic I should aspire to be?
The world can get along well without me.

Why should I study subjects I hate?
Why in History so many dates?
Why am I forced so much to learn,
Material useless, my living to earn?
Why study the plantation economy,
Or tragic misdeeds of humanity?

Many I know, who little talent did show,
Yet much do they own; not a penny do they owe.
What if at the books we all do succeed,
Who would follow, if we all could lead?
Why sacrifice today's teenage fun,
Knowing that tomorrow I'll have little or none?

Why struggle to become a renowned scientist,
Or a researcher; a Constitutional specialist?
People like these you rarely ever see,
They live a life of obscurity.
Teen years are years to be devoted to fun,
Not years to discuss elections I might one day run.

Jimmy, my child, it is good to see,
You are thinking about what you might someday be.
It is good to see, you have made a start,
In this life each must play a part.
Many prepared but did not know,
How fate had planned it; how their lives would go.

Fun in life you certainly will find,
When your concern is the improvement of the mind.
Do the best at whatever you can.
Don't live to be just another, 'I also ran'.
Life has its way of paying handsome rewards
To those who early played the right cards.

Jimmy, my boy, you are too young to see,
The problems we have as a community.
History has dealt us a very bad hand,
The effects of which you need to understand.
From kings and queens in our own country
We were brought and sold as common property.

So it was for over three hundred years,
We watered the earth with blood, sweat, and tears.
Constantly deprived of basic human rights,
Always aware of the planter's might.
Day after day to the fields we would go,
Remembering the stories of Timbuktu.

Jimmy, my boy, my advice to you,
Your work in school please diligently do.
Do your work to the highest quality,
Never should you settle for mediocrity.
Take my advice my dear grandson,
Academic success is the greatest fun.

I Am A Very Special Person

I am a very special person as everyone can see,
There is no one on this planet exactly like me.
There is something I know better than anyone else,
I know more about the story of myself.

I was born to make a special contribution.
No one else can do it! Only I can.
First I must prepare myself
To be the best that I can ever be.

I shall not allow anything to stop me,
From becoming what I want to be.
Myself I must learn to respect,
If the respect of others I expect to get.

I shall be honest in thought, word, and deed,
My behavior shall be exemplary.
I must have a goal in life
Even though I might live with strife.

I shall work towards my life's goal
And achieve it long before I am old
I must be careful of strangers I meet,
Tragedy too often follows deceit

With classmates and teachers I must work without rest,
To make my school the nation's best.
Change this nation I must believe I can,
Substantial change begins with one.

Beautiful, Beautiful Butterfly

Beautiful, beautiful butterfly
Please tell me; please tell me why;
Why do you fly up to the sky?
Moving about from place to place,
In all your splendor with so much grace.

My curious friend, you may not see . . .
But I am always busy at my duty.
My job is one I do enjoy.
I chase away sadness and replace it with joy.
I am as happy as a child with his toy.

Carefree I move from place to place
With so much dignity and so much grace.
Day to day if you stop, you'll see . . .
Powerful messages to humanity.
Messages to you and messages to me.

A special quality I exemplify when I fly . . .
In good times and bad times; fly up to the sky.
I want the world always to see,
What a joy it is, always to be free.
My freedom I wish I could share with thee.

Beautiful, beautiful butterfly
An important lesson I have learnt from thee.
True happiness I'll find, when I learn to be . . .
Peaceful and graceful, aspiring always, to be truly free.
Such is the source of inner beauty . . .
Such will be my eternal philosophy.

We Are One!!
To All People Of African Descent
Nationalist Movements and African Independence

We are one! Oh children of Africa—
Scattered throughout the Diaspora.
Separated we are by land and sea,
The tragic result of history.
Focused we are on nationality,
Contrary to the thoughts of Marcus Garvey.
These were his words to you and to me,
"One God! One aim! One destiny!"

Yes, dear reader

Over the last 500 years Africans were taken from their homeland where some were Kings and Queens, warriors and wise men (depending on their culture type). Some were traders and farm hands, some were scholars, achieving much in fields such as law and medicine, geography, mathematics and science. One source claims that some doctors had so advanced their art of surgery that they performed operations not done in Europe till 250 years later.

Such were the levels of intellectual achievement at the universities at Geo, Jenne and Timbuktu during the reign of Askia the Great. As a result of the development of slavery Africans were forced to give up their hundreds of languages, cultural practices and conform to a way of life prescribed by the masters on New World plantations.

With the development of the slave trade, places like Timbuktu and Gao once known for their achievement in scholarship 300 years later became leading markets for trade in slaves. As a historian put it, "Towns like Timbuktu and Kano retained their prosperity. The horses, required for the slave raids, were purchased by means of slaves; one horse being valued at twelve to fifteen slaves depending on the age and sex of the slave."

Not until 15,000,0000-20,000,000 Africans were removed from the continent on the Trans Atlantic slave trade did the slave trade come to an end. The next step in European involvement in Africa was what came to be called 'The Partition of Africa'. The entire continent with the exception of Ethiopia came under European control. These European countries included Spain, France, Germany, Portugal, Italy, Belgium and Britain.

237

The next stage in African development was the age of Nationalism and Nationalist Movements. Good examples of African leaders of the period were Kwame Nkrumah of Ghana, Jomo Kenyatta of Kenya, Felix Houphouet Boigny, who had been leader of the Ivory Coast for many years, became president of the Ivory Coast after it achieved independence in 1960, Nelson Mandela, who after serving twenty six years imprisonment for treason under the racist apartheid government became President of South Africa, and for the first time, brought true democracy to the South African people as a whole.

Africa! Oh Africa!

Africa! Oh Africa! Birthplace of humanity,
Africa! Dear Africa! Land of much controversy.
Good Mother that thou art, you have given from your heart—
Your wisdom and children; you've played your part.

The greatness of Egypt, some have tried to deny,
Though this is impossible, they continue to try.
Science and art are among your contributions,
To the things you've given to Western civilization.

Africa! Oh Africa! What's in a name!
Your true place in History 'tis time to reclaim.
Your children have awakened joyfully at last,
To make known to the world, the truth of your past.

Africa! Oh Africa! Land of variety
Of climate and animals—everywhere you see.
Mountains and deserts your borders do embrace,
Grassland and forest each in its place.

Africa! Oh Africa! Great
Empires you once had,
Memories of which, make the heart glad.
Ghana, Songhai and ancient Mali
Were centers of trade, and much industry.

Africa! Oh Africa! These are some names
Of men of distinction, of men of great fame.
Mansa Musa of Mali, great Emperor was he,
Great warrior, state builder was Sonni Ali.

Askia the Great was a very special man,
For his state, Songhai—he had a good plan.
At Gao, Walata and Timbuktu,
He build universities, not just for a few.

From Europe and Asia many scholars did come,
To obtain knowledge they had not at home.
Africa! Dear Africa! Be of good cheer!
The truth of thy past will be taught again.

Africa! Dear Africa! Don't indulge your pain.
Africa, Oh Africa! Africa, Dear Africa!
You shall be great again.
Yes! You shall be great again.

A Reason To Smile

I am African!
I am the embodiment of thousands of years of culture!
My individuality finds expression through my community
I am a part of the great circle of life.
I respect the earth, the animals, the trees and all mankind.
I am African; I am known for my dignity and pride.
I have a reason to smile.

I am abused!
Deprived of my freedom! Stacked like cargo!
Transported over rough seas; subjected to sub-human conditions.
I lie with filth, disease and grief. Daily I live with death;
I see pain and terror in my people's eyes.
I am African! I have survived!
I have a reason to smile.

I am for sale!
I am stripped, shaved and oiled!
I am placed on the auction block and sold like common stock.
I see terror in beautiful eyes! What horror does the future hide?
I am guardian of a valuable treasure—my African culture.
I am African! I have survived!
I have a reason to smile.

I am property!
I live to be used and abused; to suffer and die.
My culture is suppressed; my creativity destroyed.
I rise when I am told! I'll do it till I grow old.
I am father; I am mother! Yet, no son or daughter.
I am African! I have survived!
I have a reason to smile.

I am a tool!
I exist to be exploited! I can be bought or sold.
I am thought of as inferior; I am at the mercy of a foreign master.
Even if I am freed, a slave's life I will lead.
I have no legal rights; I'd prefer death to a life like this.

I am African! I have survived!
I have a reason to smile.

I am important!
I am the producer of wealth; the main stay of Southern economy
I am the source of controversy and Sectional rivalry.
I am the reason for compromise.
I am at the center of this nation's history.
I am African! I have survived!
I have a reason to smile.

I am used!
I am at the center of conflict.
My fate hangs on a political game! I am emancipated!
I have served my purpose, I am neither citizen nor slave.
I am a person! A person without rights.
I am African! I have survived.
I have a reason to smile.

I am free!
I am given a helping hand, I am able to achieve.
I am part of the political plan
I am a threat! I have proven that I can!
I am ambitious! I am as good as anyone else!
I am African! I have survived.
I have a reason to smile.

I am an American
I am granted citizen and human rights.
I use them well! I am a political threat!
I will be stopped! Again I am an object of compromise.
My privileges are withdrawn. I am the subject of hate.
I am American! I have survived.
I have a reason to smile.

I am a semi-slave.
I am a social reject.
I work like a slave; I get nothing in return
I am lynched and shot, because I am black.
The system is against me. To whom can I turn?
Am I American really? I have survived.
I have a reason to smile.

I am a fighter.
I served in two World Wars, I am loyal and patriotic.
At home I am still a semi-slave; daily used and abused

I must fight back! Enough is enough!
I must take a stand! I must change this land.
I am an American! I have survived.
I have a reason to smile.

I am a citizen!
I must regain my rights! The courts I will use.
Confrontations and protests; sufferings and death!
Equal opportunity must be mine! I have paid the price.
I am denied Civil Rights; I will continue to fight.
I am an American! I have survived.
I have a reason to smile.

I have arrived!
I have changed the laws! I have won my Civil Rights
I am told I am free to rise to the top.
I am lawyer, doctor, professor, leader and spiritual guide.
I am dispossessed; I am delinquent; homeless; ignored.
I am African American! I have survived.
I have a reason to smile.

I am misunderstood.
I am unemployed, I am harassed and imprisoned
I am a person, a parent, a friend, a child!
I too have dreams, I breath, I feel! I love, I cry!
I hope that I will be understood and accepted for who I am.
I am African American! I have survived.
I have a reason to smile.

I am the past, I am the present.
I have been abused, I have survived.
I am human, I am important.
I am African, I am American.
I am citizen, I have earned my rights.
I am **President,** I have a good reason to smile.
I am African American, The future is mine.
Yes! The future is mine.

References

Augier, F.R., Gordon, S.C., Hall, D.G., Record, M., <u>The Making of the West Indies</u>, Great Britain: Longmans, Green and Co Ltd, 1960

Carter, E.H., Digby, G.W., Murray, R.N. <u>History of the West Indian Peoples, 18th Century to Modern Times</u>, Hong Kong: Thomas Nelson and Sons Ltd, 1954

Carter, E.H., Digdy, G.W., Murray, R.N. <u>History of the West Indian Peoples, From Earliest Times to the 17th Century</u>; Great Britain: Thomas Nelson and Sons Ltd, 1959

Craton, Michael. <u>A History of the Bahamas</u>, Great Britain: Collins Clear-Type Press, 1962

Crowder, Michael, <u>The Story of Nigeria</u>, London: Faber and Faber, 1962

Danzer, Gerald A., Klor de Alva, J. Jorge., Wilson, Louis E., Woloch, Nancy, <u>The Americans</u>, McDougal Littell, 1998

DaSilva, Benjamin, Finkelstein, Milton, Loshin, Arlene, Sandifer, Hon. Jawn A. <u>The Afro-American in United States History</u>, New York, New York: Globe Book Company, Inc, 1969

Globe Book Company, Consultants: Harley, Sharon, Middleton, Stephen, Stokes, Charlotte M., <u>United States</u>: Globe Book Company, A Division of Simon & Schuster, 1992

Graham, Tom. <u>Kingston 100 1872-1972</u>. Kingston, Jamaica: Tom Graham Publications Ltd

Greenwood, R., Hamber, S. <u>Arawaks to Africans</u>, London and Basingstoke: Macmillan Publishers Ltd, 1980

Greenwood, R., Hamber S. <u>Emancipation to Emigration</u>, London and Basingstoke: Macmillan Education, 1980

Hussey, W.D., <u>Discovery Expansion & Empire</u>. Great Britain: University Printing House, Cambridge, 1966

Johnson, Doris L. <u>The Quiet Revolution in the Bahamas</u>. Nassau, Bahamas: Family Island Press Limited, 1972

Murray, Tom. <u>Folk Songs of Jamaica</u>, London: Oxford University Press, 1951

Pooley, Robert C., <u>England in Literature</u>, USA: Scott, Foresman and Company, 1953

Rubel, David. The Coming Free, <u>The Struggle for African-American Equality</u>; United States, DK Publishing, Inc., 2005

Tucker, Thomas, Ph.D. <u>From Auction Block to Glory, The African American Experience</u>, New York, NY: Michael Friedman Publishing Group, Inc, 1998

Murray, R.N. <u>Nelson's West Indian History</u>, London: Thomas Nelson and Sons Ltd, 1971

About The Author

The author, Lloyd E. Afflick was born and raised in Portland, Jamaica. He is a graduate of the Mico Teachers College and the University of the West Indies, Kingston, Jamaica. He holds a Masters Degree in Education from Florida Atlantic University, where he received a special award for Academic Excellence. He is an amateur poet and enjoys writing on social, educational and historical themes.

Throughout his long teaching career he has taught Primary, Middle and High School students in Jamaica, the Bahamas and Broward County, Florida. He is a former lecturer at the San Salvador Teacher's College, Bahamas and part-time lecturer at the College of the Bahamas, Nassau.

He was, until he retired from his position as Resource Teacher, attached to the Multicultural Department of the Broward County School Board and a guest lecturer at the Florida Atlantic University, Boca Raton, Florida. His area of specialization is History and the Social Sciences.

WE ARE ONE!!

We are one! Oh children of Africa—
Scattered throughout the Diaspora.
Separated we are by land and sea,
The tragic result of history.
Focused we are on nationality,
Contrary to the thoughts of Marcus Garvey.
These were his words to you and to me,
"One God! One aim! One destiny!"

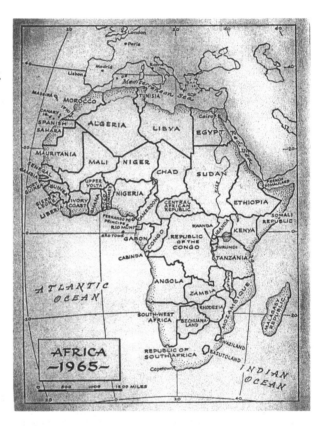